For Love or Money

A Guide to Bungee Jumping Through Life

Annie Oeth

A traditional publisher
with a non-traditional approach to publishing

Copyright © 2014 Annie Oeth

Cover Photo Credit: © 2014 Melanie Thortis

All rights reserved. WARNING: Unauthorized duplication or downloading is a violation of applicable laws, including U.S. Copyright law. File sharing is allowed only with those companies with which James L. Dickerson or Sartoris Literary Group has a written agreement.

SARTORIS LITERARY GROUP
www.sartorisliterary.com

CONTENTS

Foreword ... 9

Part I : Love, Relationships and Other Mushy Stuff

Don't leave the house without mascara ... 19
Valentine's Day ... 23
Online dating sites (may they rot in hell) ... 26
Fairy tales ... 32
The Pitch ... 36
Cats, otherwise known as a man repellant ... 40
Know what you want ... 43
Men want to be saved ... 47
Hooters ... 50
Cougars ... 53
Sexting ... 57
How to look hot ... 59
Your girls ... 61
Catch and release ... 64
Wildebeests ... 67
Men who can't spell ... 70
Purse holders ... 73
The horrors of marriage ... 76
Wasbands ... 81
Doing nothing ... 84
Men Worth Having ... 86
Forcing roses ... 88
The right one ... 92
The Kids ... 94
Marriage ... 98

Rules of engagement ... 101
I can't wait no more ... 105
Wedding planning ... 108
Happily ever after ... 112
It's not about the ring ... 114

Part II: Money and Other Reasons To Holler

Don't settle ... 119
Digging out ... 122
Patterns ... 126
Credit cards (may they burn in hell) ... 132
Bills, bills, bills ... 136
Broke but not broken ... 140
The Pink Mafia ... 144
Finding a sugar daddy ... 150
Winning the lottery ... 154
Cheap retail therapy ... 158
Get professional help ... 160
Thrift shopping ... 164
Sweaty T-shirts ... 167
Thinking rich thoughts ... 172

Part III: Living Well and Taking a Few

Leaps of Faith ... 177
Jelly ... 181
Choose to be happy ... 185
Make your own happiness ... 188
Treat yourself well ... 194
Take care of yourself ... 198

Butterfly effect ... 201
Time management ... 205
I'm rubber, you're glue ... 208
Bits and pieces ... 210
Pinch off the suckers ... 213
Codependence Day ... 216
The blessing of being blessed ... 219
Give them something to talk about ... 222
Predict the future (by creating it) ... 226
Afraid to fail, afraid to succeed ... 229
Wake up already ... 232
Take the leaps ... 239
Parting thoughts ... 242

Acknowledgements

Foreword

Writing about love and money, or for that matter, bungee jumping, was a natural choice for me since I have such a stellar track record in love, money and doing things that scare the crap out of me.

If there was a sarcasm font, I would have typed that sentence in it.

Dealing with love and money is hard. Few people do both well. Some can handle money, and others are blessed with healthy relationships, and then there are those who struggle with both. The problems with money fuel arguments in relationships, and sometimes unhealthy relationships can wreck your finances.

Just having one or the other would be pretty awesome, but being single—or worse, in a bad relationship—and then being broke is a great big Margarita glass full of awful.

When you are broke and broken-hearted, you can't even buy good chocolate to take the sting out of whatever made your train to happily ever after jump the tracks. When you are broke and your heart got stomped on by someone's pair of Cole Haans, you can't afford to put a Band-Aid on it with a little retail therapy.

Love and money have been twin failures for me more often than not, but at least I have company. You have problems with men and money, and you are guaranteed a large group of fellow women who will drink with you on girls' night out.

I like to add a "so far" at the end. Love and money have been twin failures for me more often than not, so far. Hope springs eternal.

It honestly doesn't seem fair to have problems with love and money at the same time.

One train wreck at a time.

But no, when it rains, it pours, ladies.

Sometimes I have had the trifecta of lacking love, money and time, all at once, and I know I can't be the only one with that much bad karma.

Yet love and money shape the course of our lives. One affects the other, and they often impact the lives of those closest to us.

Showing a little wisdom here is called for. Not only that, but respect.

Every January 1 for the last several years, my New Year's resolution has been to respect myself in every way possible. Respecting myself means keeping myself healthy by moving enough to accelerate my heart rate and taking vitamins and saving the greasy cheeseburgers for special occasions. It means allowing myself time to think and read and pray and just be still and quiet. It means giving myself a little shove professionally, and saving for my future and the futures of my sweet babies.

When it comes to love and money, respect for yourself is key. After all, if you don't respect yourself, who else is going to?

In relationships, respect for yourself means you are not going to put up with a man you can't count on, or worse, one you *can* count on … to yell at you or your sweet babies, to disrespect you and to be less than you deserve. Being alone is miles better than being in a relationship that disrespects who you are and the person God created you to be.

When it comes to money, respect for yourself means respecting your money. It means being organized with it, and having a plan.

Think of those you love. Think of how you would want their money situation to be. You'd want them to not be stressed, and to have what they need plus more.

Now think of yourself and your own situation. If you love yourself, which you should, then you should want this same situation, not just enough to wish for it but enough to take steps to make it your reality.

I will be the first to say that, in the past, I have not respected myself in these areas.

I tried to make bad relationships into good ones.

(Spoiler alert: This almost never works.)

Part of my life, I lived robbing Peter to pay Paul if Paul was the bank or the electric company and Peter owned MasterCard.

Worse, I have managed to combine a bad relationship and money trouble, and even when I tried to make things better, they got worse. Trying to make money problems better, without someone else's buy-in, only gets you more problems, plus resentment later on.

There is a fine line between helping someone you love and being codependent with someone you love. Trying to fix problems for someone is an unhealthy substitute for encouraging them to fix their own problems. The latter will leave that person feeling healthy and empowered, and the former will leave that person feeling gratitude for a day or so, followed by resentment forever.

I have had good intentions, but you know what they say about those. They're the pavers Satan uses for his patio.

And then there is bungee jumping. I've never had the desire to do so literally, and for the life of me, I can't understand why someone would pay someone else to let them bungee jump.

It looks terrifying.

There's the first fall, but if that isn't scary enough, you then come to the end of your bungee cord and bounce up, and then down, and then up and then down.

Some couples decide to bungee jump after they recite their wedding vows. As if marriage wasn't terrifying enough.

Figuratively, though, we all bungee jump. Sometimes we're shoved into it, and sometimes we get a running start and leave the ground of our own volition, but we all take risks and take leaps of faith.

We have to, and no matter how scary the bungee jumps are, not jumping, not taking some chances in life, is a bigger risk than the leaps.

No risks, no gains. I don't know about you, but I would rather look back on my life as having taken chances and fallen down a few times along the way than wonder what would have happened if I had made those leaps of faith.

Taking chances on relationships and goals works out better if you do the right things, but you learn by making mistakes.

I am writing this book as an expert in doing the wrong things. It's a journey for me. A project, if you will.

And I have plenty of those. I love a good project.

Our home is one continuous project.

Once the dining room is painted, the kitchen is being measured for new counters. The outside could use a new coat of white, the color my daddy always favored for houses. He swore it kept the house cooler, but I think the air conditioner does that.

It's one thing after another.

At our house and with myself.

I work on myself, too. My exercise used to be running to the refrigerator during commercials, but now I love walking with friends and going for a run.

I used to say I had no time to read, but I've managed to read about four or five books a month for the last several years.

I didn't think I had time to write and hold down a full-time job, but ... ta-da!

All kinds of things can be done, bit by bit, step by step.

The love and money part, I'm also working on.

When it comes to money, I realize as a single parent I have a heavy load. My dealings with money have been too haphazard. Sometimes I have avoided looking at my bank balance just because I don't want to know.

By the grace of God, we're in our home and two of the four kids have college degrees, including one with a master's. Two more will have them before all's said and done.

I like to say we're the best educated, poorest family around.

All too often, though, I have used my circumstances of being a widow as a reason for not doing more and trying more.

Several years back, I decided that needed to end. I have this one chance to do my best as a parent and as a person. I don't want to ever look back and wish I had tried harder and taken more chances. I like the idea of looking back and knowing I did my best.

None of this is easy. Not love, not money and definitely not bungee jumping.

But if it was easy, any idiot could do it.

I figure anyone with a big checkbook could fund big dreams.

Any idiot could send children to college and fix up her home if she had the money in the bank to cover it.

However, it takes some creativity, discipline and nerve to fund big dreams if your name is not Mrs. Bill Gates.

Take pride in your struggles, romantic or financial, because you have not lived this many years to quit now.

No one ever gained wisdom from things coming easily to them.

At this rate, I am just loaded with wisdom, by the way. Jealous?

A struggle is a gift, and it keeps on giving, because no struggle ever leaves you the same.

Likewise, in my own faith journey, I have discovered that God isn't happy until I am doing things that terrify me.

Over and over again, I have found myself in scary situations. Some have been blessings, such as new career opportunities, but others have been brought on by losing close family members and raising four children on my own.

It is interesting that life events that could be termed as either positive or negative, something to celebrate or something to mourn, are equally terrifying. They can also involve a near-equal amount of struggle.

Blessings and tragedies can be scary and can involve work and struggle.

Spoiler alert: Life's not easy. It can be a struggle.

But struggle isn't such a bad thing. We might fear it almost as much as bungee-jumping into space, but it's a learning experience. It shapes us into who we are.

After a challenge and a struggle, after having the bejeezus scared out of you, you come out smarter.

You have a better sense of what you want, and if you don't know how to get there, you will know how *not* to get there.

You flex muscles, emotional ones and physical ones, and you get stronger.

Bit by bit, you find out you don't scare as easily as you used to.

And one day, the struggles won't feel quite as difficult. And then they won't be struggles at all.

You'll have your finances and your life in order right about the time Prince Charming shows up.

Only, because none of this came easily, you'll be smart enough not to settle, financially or romantically.

No fools or fool's gold for you.

Be brave.

Be strong.

Be blessed.

Treat yourself with respect, and build yourself a life you love with those you love.

—**Annie Oeth**

Part I

Love, Relationships and Other Mushy Stuff

Don't leave the house without mascara

Forget clean underwear. If I am going to be in an accident, let the doctor at the ER be entranced by my volumized eyelashes, and I hope I have the strength left to bat them a little.

Ladies, how else are you going to meet a doctor? I'm not advocating being reckless just so you can meet the M.D. of your dreams, but who knows? You have to be ready for the curveballs life throws you.

There was a Bible story, one of Jesus' parables, my mother would read me as a little girl. I loved it because it had bridesmaids in it, which made it sort of like a theological Disney princess story.

In the parable, there were some bridesmaids who were supposed to keep their lamps burning for when the bridegroom showed up and the party began. Some of the bridesmaids didn't bring enough oil for their lamps and went off to get some more. Of course, they got locked out of the wedding reception.

When I was growing up, preachers would use that story as a way of saying we all needed to straighten up and be ready because Jesus was coming back and would not be amused at our shenanigans. This would be followed by 15 stanzas of "Just As I Am" and a few life rededications to Christ.

That wasn't what I got out of the story as a girl.

My take on it was that you should be ready, prepared better than a Boy Scout, for life's banquets.

You can't show up to life without your mascara, because once you realize your lashes are a little low on volume, it's too late. Your friend's new hubby will haul off and lock you out of the reception while you're over at the CVS getting your Maybelline Dial-a-lash.

The other thing I thought about all that was that the bridegroom in the story was sort of being a jerk, locking them out of the party for not having their lamp oil. Seriously, if one of my girlfriends remarries, I would hope she'd marry somebody who wouldn't lock me out of the party, because there I would be in a hideous bridesmaid's gown with nowhere to go, no chocolate fountain to dunk my strawberries in, no open bar.

The story's a tragedy on so many levels.

The moral for me from this parable was that you have to show up with some mascara on your lashes. Plan ahead and bring plenty of lamp oil, metaphorically speaking.

It's like insurance. I pay my car insurance, and I don't have a wreck. I miss a payment and let the policy lapse, and automatically, all the world's Mack trucks are trying to run me down on my way to drop a check off at the insurance office.

If I have some long, black, volumized whopper lashes, then I will be seen by the normal people I usually see. They will see me, we say hi, drink coffee, work and go home. Life is good.

But let me head into work without some war paint on, and that will be the day that Johnny Depp, Sean Connery and Brad Pitt decide to walk into the newsroom.

That will be the day everyone has to get a new work ID badge photo, and I am living with the results of what happened the last time ID badge photos were made. It isn't pretty.

It is the way life works. You meet the man of your dreams on the day your hair sticks up, when all your lipstick is gone and you look like a booger in stilettos.

You just hope that he's enough man of your dreams to love you anyway. If there is a Murphy's Law, and there is, then there is also an addendum. I call it Mary Kay's Law.

If you don't have your mascara on, that will be the day Dr. McDreamy and you meet up in the ER. Of course, fate could smile on you, with mascara showing up on your lashes the same day your dream man appears.

There was a newspaper clipping years ago of a woman commenting on a new dollar store opening up. She was happy with the new store in town, saying she could just run in there and didn't have to dress up like she was going to Wal-Mart.

Yes, my city friends laughed and laughed over this, but not me.

In small town Mississippi where I grew up, you not only dressed up for Wal-Mart, but you hot-rolled your hair for Wal-Mart, and put on mascara and lip gloss, too.

Having shiny lips was key in the late 1970s and early 1980s of my youth. My lips could have glowed in the dark.

Working in the newspaper business is quite entertaining and informative. It's like free entertainment with life lessons. It's also one of the few businesses where you can sit around, drink coffee and read newspapers and be considered working. Now, in this day of social media, we're encouraged to play on Facebook and surf the 'net.

So while I was goofing around on the internet at work, I found a news story online about the number of couples who meet at Wal-Mart. It's a virtual singles bar.

Some couples even get married at Wal-Mart, which would be handy for the reception. Guests could go from the garden area ceremony to the deli counter for the reception and the beer aisle for the bar.

This just proves it. You have to be ready for anything. Your forever soul mate could be looking at plungers in the hardware section, so no going to Wal-mart without getting gorgeous first.

There is more to this cautionary tale than long, thick, black eyelashes, though.

All this eyelash-fluttering is a metaphor for being ready for good stuff to happen.

Because it will, or at least it might if you are ready for it, let it happen and see where it leads.

Act like today is going to be great, and it has a better shot of turning out that way. Believe you're going to succeed and you just improved your odds. Apply mascara like your dream man is just around the corner, because he just might be.

And if he isn't, you've at least got gorgeous volumized lashes.

Valentine's Day

The National Retail Federation says Americans spent nearly $7 billion on Valentine's Day in 2013, and I promise you that a good portion of those billions were spent in a desperate effort to not be sleeping on the couch.

Ironically, sometimes Valentine's Day can suck the romance out of things. Instead of flowers just because, there are flowers because he darned well better or else.

If you are single, Valentine's Day can feel like National Everyone Else is in a Happy Relationship but You Day, The whole rest of the world is arm in arm, smooching, all red roses and dark chocolate and romance. It's sickening, really.

Unless you happen to be in a relationship. Then Valentine's Day is glorious.

It's also a lot of pressure, because, if you have a significant other, you want to get Valentine's Day right, even if the other days go wrong. A good Valentine's Day can add up to forgiveness for future stupidity.

The expectations bar is up there. Men have the bar set higher than women do, but our bar is up there, too, ladies.

The Gentleman Friend and I started dating about a month before Valentine's Day, so then there was the question of how much to do. Spend too much, do too much and we'd frighten each other away. Do too little, and we'd both look like we didn't care. I had to figure out how to reveal my growing affection without scaring him half to death.

It's a fine line to walk, caring while trying to look like you do, just not too much. It felt like the whole future of our relationship hinged on Feb. 14.

That's a lot of pressure.

Some people just pitch the day. These are people who either aren't in relationships or flat out don't care about the relationship they are in. When the response to "What do you want to do for Valentine's Day?" is "Not a damned thing," you know your relationship is one yank away from the plug being pulled on life support.

Yes, it's just a day, and there are 364 others on the calendar, but even if you move your Valentine's Day celebration to another day in the interest of sanity and beating the crowds at the restaurants in your town, you're at least celebrating it. When Valentine's Day is flat-out ignored, not forgotten but on purpose defied, you can just bet that the next call is to the divorce lawyer.

Valentine's Day makes some people get what my mama used to call the heebie-jeebies. Those are the true believers, in love or chocolate or just pure excitement.

My mama was a teacher in her single days, dealing with 40-something first-graders in the days before there was a lower ceiling on how many children you could cram into a classroom. Her job was crowd control and teaching reading.

So what was the best day for reading and the worst day for crowd control in her classroom? Valentine's Day.

It was horrible, she said.

Worse than Halloween, Thanksgiving and Christmas rolled into one.

On Valentine's Day, every child was hopped up on sugar and chomping at the bit to see who sent them a Valentine. Duct tape and Super Glue wouldn't have kept those youngsters at their desks.

And, of course, they could read their Valentines by this time if she did her job, so these weren't mere slips of colored paper. They were messages from friends and sometimes secret admirers.

"I like you," some of the youngsters would print with their fat first-grader pencils.

Sometimes it meant "like," and sometimes it meant "like like."

"Like like" is pretty serious. You "like like" someone, and before long, you are living in the suburbs and pushing a baby stroller on the walking trails.

So no wonder their little hearts were a-twitter. Whose wouldn't be?

The best way to treat this holiday is with heartfelt expressions. Not because you are expected to, but because you want to.

It's why one of my Dear Sons would spend hours hunting for the perfect Valentine for the girl he was pretty sure he "like liked" because she could play football.

It's why I wined and dined the Gentleman Friend on our first Valentine's Day, telling him to put away his wallet. And it's why he popped for a chocolate-dipped strawberry for each day we knew each other, dipped by his own hands.

"You know, next year you are not getting 390-something strawberries," he warned.

I melted like the chocolate with the words "next year."

Online dating sites (may they rot in hell)

Back when I first started dating, boys gave girls their class rings to wear if you were going steady.

Those were simpler times, days when you would get your friend to tell his friend that if he wanted to go to the homecoming dance with you and asked, you were likely to say yes. Back then, you had your people contact his people. It was like Hollywood or international diplomacy, take your pick.

Dating in your 40s is, as I was to discover, totally different than dating in your teens. It's not like apples and oranges, or even apples and rutabagas. It's like apples and bowling balls or apples and chainsaws.

When I began dating again as a full-grown old-enough-to-know-better mother of four, I was terrified.

I should have been.

I decided to enter this brave new world by starting an account on Match.com. One of my BFFs was on eHarmony, and we would compare notes.

The first challenge is to write your profile. Don't sweat this too much because there's a good chunk of the dating population who will not read it. Some of them can read well. They just choose not to.

They go straight to the photo.

I chose a photo of myself, a selfie that I took after getting a good haircut so I would remember what it was supposed to look like once the stylist hit the final spray. I was then asked by one silver-tongued devil how many years ago that was taken and if that was me 300 pounds ago.

I wondered how on earth that man was still single. Nothing like being called a liar and accused of being fat in real life to make a girl swoon.

So I was ready to go, me, my bio and my selfie. The bait was in the water, and it was time to reel in my dream dates.

One of my dream date potentials turned out to be a white supremacist.

Jealous?

Seriously, I would have taken his profile as a huge politically incorrect joke at first. He was looking for a blue-eyed blonde woman of European extraction about 20 years younger than he, fertile, submissive and wealthy through a trust fund.

And yet he was emailing me. Because except for European part and being a female, that was not now me and never was. A dark-eyed brunette at least as old or older, with more month than money and no interest in birthing any more babies was not about to fit his bill.

Match.com has this handy "block" feature that I learned to use.

Then I chatted by phone with another man. He was divorced, funny, smart. So far, so good, right?

And then he drunk dialed me. Then he called a few days later to drunk apologize for the first drunken call.

I have issues but a good relationship with the right woman would fix me, he said during the drunken apology.

Ladies, when a man says anything close to what I just paraphrased, run.

Run like a rabid beast is after you, only worse.

Because what is really behind you is a rabid beast with a black hole of need that will suck you in, maybe along with your credit cards.

I don't recall exactly what I said, but it was something to the tune of, "I am raising four children. I don't have the energy to fix you."

Nor the inclination, but I am Southern enough not to be ugly about it.

Besides, I swore off fixer-uppers. If your fixer-upper is a house, it has character. If your fixer-upper is a man, he may not and probably doesn't.

Then there was the time I was checking out a dating website for my eHarmony-using girlfriend.

I had been dating someone steadily but not seriously, and lo and behold, there he was on the site, active within the past 24 hours. And there were other men there who I happened to know were in relationships, also active in the past day or so.

They immediately were added to my list of Men Not Worth Having.

So yes, there are things about online dating that make your cats, the sofa, Netflix and a carton of Blue Bell look wonderful in comparison.

But the horror stories go both ways.

Men should keep a list of Women Not Worth Having, because there's quite a few of them. Sorry if I am stomping on some toes, ladies.

A male friend told me of the woman he began seeing after meeting on Match.com. Things were going along swimmingly until she let it slip that she was currently married.

Not as in married but going through a divorce and it is fixing to be final any day now.

Not as in separated.

Not as in married but I sent him out for a half-gallon of milk three years ago and he hasn't shown back up since.

Nope, "married" as in living in the same house, sleeping in the same bed and filing a joint tax return.

"Why didn't you tell me this?" my friend asked.

"Because I didn't think it would matter," he said she replied.

There are all kinds of things that wouldn't have mattered to my friend. Hair color? No biggie. Baptist or Methodist? Not a big deal.

Married, though, was sort of a deal breaker on dating. Other than the breaking of a commandment or two, there was the problem of imagining an angry husband ready to shoot first and ask questions later.

Another story I heard involved a woman who broke up with her online beau because he had not proposed marriage yet. This was after three months. Not years, not decades, but months.

Men, it turns out, do not have the "crazy" market cornered. Whatever the boys can do, the girls can, too. Good, bad and ugly.

I had to swear off the online dating services. There were lots of first dates for me, but not many second ones. Apparently, I make an awesome first impression. One date with me, and they head for the hills or join the Witness Protection Program.

That and there was so much small talk involved. Enough that I felt like making a resume to hand out at the first date. There are only so many times a person wants to chat about favorite colors, movies and restaurants.

It was also tiring informing friends that I would be meeting someone for the first time for a cup of coffee and that if I didn't answer my phone, they should assume my online date was a serial killer.

Most men I met online are good people and most of them are friends of mine today, but there just weren't sparks flying from either of us on our dates. We all wished each other well.

I did recoup some of my online dating membership fees through eating out. I had a couple of Japanese dinners, a lunch or two and a sit-down dinner here and there, plus the odd cup of coffee, so I'm calling it even.

Fairy tales

When I was a little girl, I loved princesses and fairy tales. We girls all did.

When bedtime came, I would beg for just one more story. I'd snuggle down into the covers and start imagining the castles and ball gowns and knights and shining armor. Life was going to be awesome, I'd think. One love-at-first-sight ga-ga glance across the ballroom, and I would be on my way to happily-ever-afterville.

The problem, though, is that little boys aren't always clued in on these fairy tales. They're all into killing giants and slaying dragons. It's like they missed the whole happily-ever-after part. Give them a big sword, and they're happy.

Little boys aren't told the same night-night stories little girls are. I know, and I am guilty here, because I didn't read my sons princess stories.

Their favorites were "The Cat In The Hat," which is about messing up the house and hiding the evidence, and "Jack And The Beanstalk," which is about trading the family cow for magic beans, killing a giant who lives in the sky and taking his stuff.

These two stories explain so much about boys and men. It's all about the art of the deal, slaying something bigger than yourself and not getting caught by mom or a giant or a dragon. About the last thing a little boy would want to do is go live happily ever after with some girl.

Girls' stories don't necessarily have the best of lessons.

Let's take "Cinderella," for example.

Cinderella gets rescued by a Fairy Godmother instead of thinking of her own way out of her evil stepmother's house, and she falls for the first man she meets. OK, points that he is a handsome prince, but usually the first man you meet is not a royal.

They dance the night away at a ball that was thrown because Prince Charming could not find an eligible bachelorette. Let me stop right here and say that if a handsome prince who lives in a castle and is loaded with moolah can't get a date, that's a red flag.

But let me continue.

They fall in love at first sight and trip the light fantastic until the clock strikes 12. And as my daddy used to say, nothing good ever happens after midnight.

Our girl Cindy has to go running from the castle, lest the prince see her un-done-up self, dropping one of her glass slippers on the way out. These had to have been tempered glass or Lucite, or maybe some faux glass Tupperware, because I have a tile floor, and anything that can break that hits it will. Miraculously, not only do the magic shoes not break, but they didn't disappear or change back into whatever they were before.

Here are some more royal problems. The prince and Cindy fall in love at first sight. And I know that sounds super romantic, but the word that describes what the prince and Cindy were feeling is four letters long and starts with L, but it is not love.

Relationships that start with lust and attraction and fireworks and having hearts where your eyes should be can turn into love. I am romantic enough to think that many times, they do. But it takes more than a few waltzes around the ballroom for that to happen.

And the prince didn't fall for Cinderella as she was. He fell for the bibbity-bobbity-boo-ed Cinderella. The one with the "What Not To Wear" makeover.

Would he have fallen in love with the "before" Cindy?

Maybe, but he didn't get to see her until he went off, glass slipper in hand, to hunt her down.

There are some problems with this part of the story, too.

Problem number one is that Prance-some Hence, I mean Handsome Prince, is in love with her, danced this close with her, stared into her beautiful eyes ... and to find her, he has to see if her foot fits in the slipper she dropped.

He can't recognize her face? Yet he is head over heels. With her feet.

The prince is smitten enough, that, once the shoe fits, he whisks Cinderella off to the castle to get hitched. After one date.

And they live happily ever after. Realistic, no?

And then there is "Sleeping Beauty," in which Princess Aurora goes off into the woods to sing and scamper around with a basket pretending to gather twigs or berries or whatever it is that princesses gather out in the forest, and she meets the prince.

Because that's where princes hang out ... the forest.

The four-letter L word hits, and they are in love, or a similar four-letter word starting with L.

You can tell because, in the Disney movie, they sing together and they're both among the beautiful people of the kingdom. Pretty people don't sing to each other unless they are in L-word territory.

This is an excellent message we send little girls: Don't talk to strangers. Unless they're hot.

If, and only if, their level of hotness hits the Prince Charming level, it is then permissible to sing to each other on the first date.

Then there is "The Little Mermaid."

In this story, Ariel, a princess in her own right, gives up her own identity to run off after Prince Eric. I don't care if you have singing crustaceans, this is not a good message for anyone, male, female, boy, girl or amphibian.

No one should give up who they are. As an Alabama friend of mine once said, "There's a lid for every jar." Don't change the jar you are to make someone else's lid fit.

Here's the big thing, though: Happily ever after may describe some things, but marriage is not one of them.

Marriage is hard. Grueling, even.

Sometimes your prince is out of work. Sometimes the kids are sick or the castle needs repairs. Girls who grow up to be women expecting a storybook romance find out the difference between fiction and nonfiction. In some cases, pretty darned quick.

Maybe there should be a few new stories, where the princess slays her own dragon and isn't rushed down the aisle to marry a handsome guy she's just met.

And maybe they live happily ever after, not because they're hot, not because they're wealthy and not because they're wearing crowns in a castle, but because they share a friendship as well as a love that grew over time.

The Pitch

Everyone's got one. Or perhaps several.

In baseball, there's the slider, the fastball, the curveball.

Car salesmen pitch you a line about the newest model, or maybe last year's style or an old clunker. It's whatever he says to make you want to sign on the dotted line, just like the pitcher hopes his pitch will bring on a swing that's ill-timed.

For single men and women, it's their stories. Who they are, what they do, how they got here and where they are going. They're pitching, and each pitch is as unique as the pitcher, salesman or saleswoman.

There are some pitchmen and pitchwomen out there who rehearse this stuff, and their pitches may not be any more related to the truth than I am to the Queen of England.

And then there are those who take the novel approach of telling the truth. Some are selective, telling the "good" truth and shoving the bad and ugly facts to the back of the closet and slamming the door.

And some just throw it all out there like it's a 10-for-$1 table at a yard sale, and you can sort through it, separating the trash from the treasure.

For years and years, I had no pitch at all. Married folks don't, or shouldn't. Watch out for the ones who are out pitching when they should be safe at home. And yes, some are bold enough to wear their wedding band when they throw their pitches.

After becoming single again, I decided to be open to the idea of dating. And that meant listening to all kinds of pitches. Here are a few of the notable ones:

The Future CEO: This guy wants to wow you with money. Even if he is assistant night manager at the corner convenience store, he wants you to be blinded by his success in the marketplace. He either wants it known he would be excellent husband material, or just wants you to think that, never mind that marriage is the last thing on his agenda. Most likely, it's the latter.

The Traveler: This guy gets around. He will tell you about every place he has ever gone, hoping this plants the thoughts of traveling with him into your head. Even if the closest he gets to going anywhere is watching The Travel Channel from the recliner in his double-wide. It's more entertaining to listen to Johnny Cash's "I've Been Everywhere."

The Christian: I throw this in because I have gone to a couple of Christian singles events. This is the guy whose opening line is, "What church do you go to?" It is the evangelical version of "What's your sign?"

The Old-Fashioned: This guy is quite endearing. He's the man who will go old-school on you and ask if he can call on you sometime. He might show up on your doorstep with flowers.

The Let Me Whisk You Away: This is a great pitch, because women love being whisked away. How many boxes of bubble bath were sold from those "Calgon, take me away" commercials? How many of us turned into puddles when Richard Gere whisked Debra Winger away at the end of *An Officer and a Gentleman*? The caution here is that once you have been whisked away, this guy probably doesn't have the slightest idea what to do with you.

The I'm A Mess But The Right Woman Could Fix Me: Start running, ladies, and fast, when you hear that pitch. But so many of us are soft-hearted, wanting to be the one who could fix up Mr. Brooding-and-Troubled. Get this in your heads: The only one we can fix is our own selves, and even that is iffy at times. Men who are broken are broken because they haven't gotten around to fixing themselves yet. You cannot do it for them, and you cannot fix someone who doesn't want to be fixed. End of lecture.

The My Wife Doesn't Understand Me: OK, I lied. The lecture is not over. I have heard this way too many times. My response is, "That's unfortunate," followed by getting the heck away and offering up a prayer for the Mrs.

The Direct Approach: I wonder if this works on anyone, but apparently it does or men wouldn't throw this pitch. They will tell you they only want one thing, and it is not a dinner companion. Add this one to the list of Men Not Worth Having, but at least the men who throw this pitch are honest.

Women have their own arsenal of pitches, too. They include a few classics:

The Shy Girl: This with a few furtive glances says, "I'm interested" without involving a pounce.

The Flirt: Shy girl only with pounce added and shyness removed. Tequila might be involved.

The Career Girl: This girl should meet the Future CEO. She worked hard for her victories in the office and will show them off. She could be Manager of the Quarter and Girlfriend of the Year, depending on how she can balance her personal life with work.

The Athlete: Chase this girl and you will only catch her if she lets you. With active living growing more popular, some singles flaunt their 5K times or distance runs when mixing and mingling. Compatibility is key here, as few things are worse than going on a running date with someone much faster or much slower than you are. Both are awkward.

The Future Wife: This one is a fairly honest pitch if there ever was one. It can also mean that this lady is just a nice person who likes to cook. It could be either or both. Men, it's up to you to figure this one out. This one eventually keeps out the male riff-raff, though, and men who don't want someone to do kind things for them will scoot. And as odd as that sounds, there are quite a few men like that out there. They complain that women are mean, yet they come undone when a woman does something thoughtful for them and shoo her away.

There are loads more pitches out there, and they are not always lies. They often are chock full of truth, with maybe a little window-dressing added. The question for singles is, is this a pitch worth a swing?

Cats, otherwise known as a man repellant

It's a stereotype. A single woman who has fifteen cats, wears cat sweaters and sits home eating out of the ice cream carton while parked on the sofa with the kitties.

Stereotypes don't just come out of nowhere, though. Somewhere in them, there is a grain of truth that got them started. They may not be true for all, but they were true for somebody at some point in time.

Somewhere there was a single woman with lots of feline fur babies. And somewhere, there were a bunch of men who hated cats.

From my time in online dating, I can tell you that the stereotype of men who hate cats is pretty darned accurate. There were men, who, when emailing me, asked me about pets. If me having four children didn't make them run off, having three cats did. A few asked me about the cats, and those men were cat people and/or men who think the prospect of meeting a good woman might be worth putting up with a few kitties.

There are people who are dog people, and then there are cat people. And, of course, there are the bi-curious who have dogs and cats. I have cats but I also have a dog. He's cat-sized and neurotic, so he's got some feline qualities.

This is based on my own non-scientific research, but I think there are more men who are dog people than men who are cat people.

My theory is that it's because men, like dogs, can be fairly simple to decode.

Why women can't understand men is that we make things too complex. What did he mean by what he said?

Is he acting like he is not interested? It's probably because he is not interested. Scratch them on the belly, feed them a good meal, and they're happy.

Cats, though, are harder to figure out. You can pet them only so many strokes, and when you go over the limit that only they know and that changes a few times each day, they will bite you.

Cats don't like just anyone. They're selective. There is a lot of truth to the saying that a person does not adopt a cat; instead, a cat adopts a person.

There's nothing you can do to make a cat like you if they have already decided they don't like you. You could dab Fancy Feast behind your ears, and they wouldn't have anything to do with you if they have already decided you are not worth pouncing on.

Cats are complex. They don't do their thinking with their stomachs. I'm not quite sure what they think with, but they won't trade you love for a bowl of Meow Mix.

Dogs are usually fine with their people spending time on the computer or reading while they are in the room, but not cats.

Cats like to be the center of attention, going so far as to lie across a book or a keyboard to get their point across. Then you can pet them and they will purr. Right up to the point that you have petted them one too many strokes, and then they will bite you.

For these reasons, not everyone understands cats. And by everyone, I mean men, for the most part.

There are men who like cats. There aren't tons of them, but they are out there. I know I will get hate emails for saying this, but the cat-loving men I have met are a little on the complex side. Just like their little furry cat brethren.

Still, you don't ever hear about single men with fifteen cats. That seems to be just a stereotype about single women.

As one of my Dear Sons once told me, "Mom, you are only a dozen cats away from being a crazy cat lady." Perpetually single, perpetually sweeping up cat hair.

I look at our kitties, one who was sneaked into the house by my daughter, one who my oldest son adopted and named for a rock star and one who I adopted rather than see her freeze out on the mid-December streets of downtown Jackson, as a way of keeping out the riff-raff.

Men who hate cats more than they are interested in you should probably hit the road. Men who are more interested in you, interested enough to ignore your cats or learn to tolerate them, are keepers.

And if your cats like him?

That's a very good sign, because cats don't like just anyone.

Know what you want

Know what you want.

Four little words, but they can make a big difference, not only in your relationships, but in your life. It's like making a pizza. If you want a pepperoni pizza, then you will need dough, pizza sauce, mozzarella cheese and pepperoni slices.

Then you come across a strawberry. This could be the most beautiful, ripe strawberry on God's green earth. It's wonderful, sweet, but doesn't have a place in your pepperoni pizza. That would be gross.

When you come across that strawberry, you have to decide whether you still want a pepperoni pizza, because you could make a dessert pizza instead.

Or you have to part with the strawberry, because you can't turn a strawberry into a piece of pepperoni.

Common sense, right?

But how many men and women who decide they want a serious committed relationship, yet waste time with someone who doesn't want that?

They hope he'll change, and just know that this is the relationship to change him. They know she'll settle down and become Suzy Homemaker (or Suzy Half-of-a-Two-Career-Couple).

But the objects of their affection don't change. And why should they?

They are the strawberries you saw when you first laid eyes on them. And the crazy thing is, usually a strawberry will just come on out and say they're a strawberry and like being a strawberry.

Not being a strawberry is something that's never entered their minds. Yet somehow we think we're going to change them.

The fact is that most of us are pickier about the produce in the supermarket than we are about the people we let into our lives.

We should have a shopping list, and we should stick to it, but most of us enter the supermarket of potential relationships hungry and with no list, meaning we'll wind up with a lousy bag of pork rinds if we're not careful. It all goes back to knowing what you want.

I've known a few men who had no clue what they wanted, but this is one of womankind's cardinal sins. A single dad friend of mine had three rules he'd teach his kids on why girls and boys are the way they are. Here are the rules about girls: 1) Girls are mean; 2) Girls don't know what they want; 3) Girls are mean because they don't know what they want.

(By the way, the rules on boys are that boys are stupid, boys lie and boys lie because they're stupid. Now you know.)

But back to the girls. There's a lot of wisdom in what my friend says. Not knowing what you want will make you mean, because you can bet your bottom dollar that whatever you wind up with when you don't know what you want will not be what you want.

It will also make you mean, or frustrated, or sad if you know what you want, know you're not getting it in the relationship you are in and yet stick around hoping things will change. Spoiler alert: They won't.

Wishing won't change people. If it did, everybody would be changing everybody else.

And what sense does it make to find someone you think is your dream man or dream woman only to want to change them. If they need changing, then hint, hint, they are not your dream man or dream woman.

If there is an "if only" in the way you describe your relationship, that's a red flag. Things would be great "if only," and fill in the blank. If there's an "if only" then things are not great.

So the thing to do, ladies and gentlemen, is first figure out what you want.

And this may change depending on life circumstances. What you wanted at twenty may not be what you want at forty, and maybe shouldn't be, but that's up to you.

Take the time away from relationships to figure out what it is that you want, and don't dive into the dating pool until you've figured that out.

At least, now you know if you are making a pepperoni pizza or a peanut butter sandwich or an ice cream sundae. Pick the food metaphor that works best for you.

Then figure out what qualities you'd love to see in your significant other. And what qualities are deal-breakers. And how big a deal-breaker some habits or traits might be.

For example, maybe you've found a brainy man who's easy on the eyes, but he drinks too much frequently. The alcohol could outweigh all the good qualities.

Or you have full custody of your young children and you've found a great gal who makes you happy yet can't stand kids. Could be a deal-breaker.

Before you take the time to know someone else, get to know yourself. Find out what you need and what you want and what would make you over-the-moon happy.

This works in your personal life as well as in your professional pursuits, monetary goals and the way you spend your time and resources, but more on that later.

Knowing what you want may not guarantee happiness in relationships or a trip down the aisle, but it may prevent some unhappy relationships and a trip to a taping of "Divorce Court."

Men want to be saved

I grew up Baptist, and no denomination or faith does an altar call quite like the Baptists do.

The pastor wants to save those brave enough to walk the center aisle.

There are all sorts of metaphors there, relationship-wise. Maybe it's not by accident that couples walk that same center aisle on the way to and from saying their "I dos."

A colleague of mine of the male persuasion tells it like this: "We men all want to be saved."

And they just know that their salvation is coming from the woman they're interested in.

Not necessarily the woman they are with now, but the next one.

The reason why, he says, is because there is a razor-thin line between saving a man—making him a better person, encouraging him to do more and be more, prompting him to be healthier or drink less or smoke less or do a few push-ups—and changing him.

Men say they want to be saved, but they don't want to be changed.

The difference between being a man's saving grace and a nag is in the beholding.

The problem here is that men who otherwise say pretty much what they mean say they want to be saved, but they really don't. They don't mean a word of it.

They'd like to do more, be more, have more, and saying that a woman can somehow save them into doing and being these things is just an out.

When doing more and being more starts feeling like work, or when they realize that their efforts are not going to work, then they can say this woman is not really saving at all. She's just nagging.

Saving men, though, that plays right into a woman's psyche.

We love the idea of being that perfect halo-wearing woman who is the one person on the planet who can save this man from his singleness.

This sounds like I don't believe in the power of change, but I do.

My belief is that people can, indeed, change, but they have to do this alone, and that goes for men and women. People have a great capacity for positive change, but bringing that positive change about is a one-man or one-woman job.

Significant others can be supportive, and should be. In fact, let me say that if you are trying to work on improving your health or bringing about success, then steer clear of those who are going to be negative.

If you need to change significant others to get away from negativity, you might have to do that. At the least, get up and leave the room when toxic talk that pulls you away from your goals is going on.

Speaking words of encouragement, though, are not the same as saving. It's the difference between being a cheerleader yelling on the sidelines and snatching the ball and running for a touchdown.

Men, make your own touchdowns. You don't need saving, and if you do, we don't want the job. We'd rather leave the saving to Jesus.

Men and women need to save themselves if they need saving. Then they bring to their relationship a wholeness and completeness. And who doesn't want that?

Hooters

Who knew men liked owls so much?

They seem to love to go to this place called Hooters and eat chicken wings and all things that are not salads and be fawned over by waitresses in tank tops and dolphin shorts. Come to think of it, that restaurant doesn't really have a lot to do with owls at all.

Hooters is where men go to be men without a woman mentioning a pipe that needs fixing or reminding him that fried things will result in a cardiac explosion. It is the grown-up version of the He-Man Woman-Haters Club. It is where men go to escape.

It's not that women can't go to Hooters. They let me in one day, and I did not have to wear a tank top and short shorts, nor did I have to glue on a mustache and deepen my voice.

I went along with two male coworkers who thought it would be hilarious to take me to the female version of no-man's land. My take on it is that the whole thing is pretty funny.

For starters, the guys at my table knew that the wait staff had switched to wearing uniforms that were all black instead of orange and white and commented to our waitress about it.

How do you know if you are spending too much time at Hooters? When you know what the waitresses wear and notice when they change the color and style.

These are the same men who couldn't tell you what their wives were wearing earlier that day. Darkening the door of Hooters apparently turns normal guys into Tim Gunn, but as my friends pointed out, only when it comes to tank tops and shorts.

Then there were men who, I think, had twin addictions. Fried food and Hooters girls. These men looked like they eat there quite often. Often enough to be in love with the Hooters girls.

They wouldn't have cared if they did have a cardiac explosion. At least they would have died happy.

I am thinking the Hooters girls could put children through college on what these guys were tipping. They knew each other by name.

And it felt sort of sad, thinking about it. I really think Hooters might have been the only place these men got female attention along with all the fried stuff their arteries could handle.

But then, these guys were happy. The Hooters girls were happy. Who was I to judge?

Heck, at the time, this was way more of a social life than I was having.

And then Captain Obvious flew in.

I was looking at my menu, figuring out what the safest thing to order would be. It wouldn't be wings, because I had to be back at work and didn't want to be wearing wing sauce.

Nope, I went for my usual go-to order on my first time in a casual eatery: A grilled chicken sandwich.

Really, unless the chicken is pink, you really can't screw up a grilled chicken sandwich. I've had some that were a trip to heaven, and others that were somewhere in purgatory, but none that went straight to hell.

But Hooters apparently felt that I truly did not understand what the restaurant theme was. So to drive it home, they served it to me on a bun.

What's a grilled chicken sandwich? A grilled boneless chicken breast on a bun, right? Well, this sandwich came with two breasts side by side, served open-face.

Well played, Captain Obvious, well played. Because I totally didn't get that this place was about breasts.

Why, I wonder, doesn't some enterprising entrepreneur make a similar spot for women?

After all, I have been to multiple girls' nights out with my besties at a particular bar just because one or several of us thought the bartender was cute. Why not a whole restaurant of cuteness?

Really, we're easy to please. They need to make the menu heavy on dark chocolate and wine and margaritas, judging from the things we women tend to go gushy over.

And then the men need to vacuum, wash the dishes, tell us how interesting our witty banter is and make eye contact with us.

Do those things, and they wouldn't even have to wear Dolphin shorts to get a tip.

Cougars

There are some things I just don't understand.

Like how a 20-something-year-old man can be attractive to a woman in her 30s, 40s or beyond.

I don't mean attractive in a movie star kind of way, because I could look at men on the big screen and decide if they're pretty or not. No, I am talking about dating these men, taking them home, having to put up with them every day. It's that part I don't get.

It's not that I don't like men in their 20s. I have two sons who are in their mid-20s, and I love them dearly. I just couldn't see dating someone like them, though.

I know you are all protesting, "But, Annie, their dirty clothes on the floor, their lack of a coherent schedule, their propensity to play "Grand Theft Auto" for five hours at a stretch … it's so attractive."

Oh, wait, none of you women to the north of 30 said that. My bad.

I knew that being a cougar was not for me when, on a night out with a girlfriend, a younger man approached me. The bar was dark, which did me lots of favors. He comes up, introduces himself and says he's new in town.

"Oh, really?" I said. "Where are you from?"

"Hattiesburg," he said.

"My son just moved from there. Graduated from Southern Miss."

"So did I. Last year."

Well, that was awkward.

So this man-child and I chit-chat some more, and he asks my marital status. I told him I am a widow, and he then tells me he's lost his father and how his mother is dealing with being a widow. Turns out she and I were around the same age. More awkwardness.

We had a sweet conversation, the man-child and I, and he reminded me for all the world of my sons. I told him to make it a point to call his mother regularly, told him he was a good son and hugged his neck goodbye when we were leaving.

Attractive? Yes. He would have been a wonderful date for someone. Just not me.

One of my rules of dating is that if I feel a need to mother a man, then I shouldn't date him.

I should just give him some cookies, pat him on the head and send him out to play.

The only other time I was approached by a much younger man was by one of my oldest son's friends who happened to have had one too many.

Liquor, like low lights, does me all kinds of favors.

The boys were having a college reunion of sorts that I walked in on when coming home from a movie and dinner.

My son was standing there in our kitchen when his friend tried to ask me out.

"Dude, that is my *mom*," he said. "That is so not cool."

I love to embarrass my children, but that has its limits. I am not going to embarrass them by dating their friends or anyone that I might could have given birth to. In the words of my oldest, that is so not cool.

Then there's the concept of time.

A girlfriend of mine started being a sho'nuf cougar, dating a man about the age of my oldest son. I told her if she took up with my boy, I could be her mother-in-law. That wasn't even funny to think about, for either of us.

So anyway, she dates this other man-child long enough to learn that he had no understanding of responsibilities or schedules.

This may be what is refreshing to some about dating much younger people, their happy-go-lucky attitude about time, but it gets old fast. Really fast.

This is a woman with children ranging from high school to elementary in age and a full-time job, plus she is pursuing a graduate degree.

Spending time with someone is quite a gift for a busy woman to give, because time is worth quite a lot. So last-minute changes of plans don't go over so well with women in their 40s because we have lives, and they are busy lives.

Play with our emotions, but don't play with our schedules. Ever.

And what on earth do you talk about?

I once worked with a younger man who was listening to a conversation about Michael Jackson I was having with a fellow coworker born around the same time I was.

We were waxing sentimental about buying his 45s with our allowance money back in the day, and he said, "I don't mean to be disrespectful, but what's a 45?"

What's a 45?

That, ladies, is what you get with a man in his 20s. Someone who has no idea what a 45 is. Someone who never dialed a phone instead of punching numbers in. Someone who can't remember life before the internet. Someone who doesn't remember when Pac Man came out.

Sure, there are bright 20-something-year-old men, witty men who can carry on an intelligent conversation, and I count my sons in that number, but they haven't walked where we walked or lived through what we lived through. They have a lot of living to do and things to experience that are going to be old hat to us just because we've been there and done that.

I suppose they could just sit there and be pretty, and they are that. And women I know who have dated younger see it as a big boost to the ego, just like the men who date younger women do. And there are some long-term relationships between men and women whose ages are, shall we say, spread apart.

But for every one of those, there are a dozen or more short-term ego boosts, sort of like a 5-Hour Energy shot to the self image.

We experienced women may love to look at the 20-something-year-old men on the movie screen, but for me, finding forever is best done with a man who knows what a 45 record is.

Sexting

If there are any men reading this, let me offer you some advice. This information will prevent you from being a laughingstock or worse.

Are you ready?

Here it is: Women are not aroused when you text them photographs of your genitals.

I know that must be hard for you men to fathom, but we really just think it is laughable. Or gross. Or both. Or worse.

I have not personally received one of these texts, and I would not like to receive one, so put your iPhones down. Read the news of the day, though, and chances are there is some famous person or elected official snapping photos south of the border and sending them to women.

And some women with more cell phone bars than sense will take photos of themselves and text them to men, and I don't mean selfies of them in Sunday school class.

And by women, I don't mean that they just turned old enough to vote. I am talking women on the back side of 40.

This, ladies, is just as bad as the men who go camera-happy and twice as stupid.

It's a depressing thought that we as a society get the amazing technology that allows us to take photographs with a phone.

What do we do with it? Create art? Solve problems?

No, we bombard others with unwanted photos of hoo-hahs and tallywhackers.

And here is the really silly part, and it gets back to the differences in wiring between men and women.

Some women believe that when they send what they believe to be private photos to a man that he will not show them to the rest of the world.

Let's just stop here and laugh uproariously. Hahahahahahahahaha. Wait, I have more laughter to get out. Hahahahahahahahaha. Let me catch my breath.

Women, if you text something visual to a man, know that he will show it to everyone up to and including God. I don't care what he tells you, if he has a Y chromosome, he is 99.9 percent likely to show off this photo.

That is the way men are. They are visual. Sometimes they think with their eyes. And other parts. Just not their brains.

It's an ego thing. They show the naughty pictures to their Y-chromosome friends, who also happen to be visual.

I have heard women all angry and broken-hearted over this happening to them, and I am sorry they are hurt, but they might as well have sent it to the world their own selves.

Hitting "send" to a man when you are sending a naughty photo is the same darned thing. You might as well put your sexting photo on a billboard on I-55.

I am willing to admit that not all men would reach this degree of badness. But if they wouldn't put it on a billboard or the equivalent, they would at least make it the wallpaper of their cellphone.

There have been people charged with crimes who sext to underage people, and this is how it should be. And I have done everything but put anti-sexting posters up in an effort to drill it into my teenagers' heads that sexting is a poor, poor choice.

Those who are old enough to know better ought to be charged with a crime. The charge would be stupidity, which might be a misdemeanor or a class A felony, depending on to whom you hit "send" for.

How to look hot

We women work at this all the time: How to look hot.

Magazines have this on the cover: "10 ways to look hot," right next to "5 ways to drive your man crazy in bed" and "12 ways to get skinny." And women from girlhood to grandmama-hood read them

It is such a moving target. Should your hair be curly or stick straight? Skinny jeans or bootcut? Heels or flats? Depends on the cycle, because just as soon as you have ballet flats in your closet, stilettos are in. Got curls? Go buy a hair straightener.

And the skincare. I used to be a soap-and-water girl until about 30 or so. Then the age-fighting weaponry came out. Moisturizer, eye serum, and what I really need is some neck wattle remover.

We start out focusing on making our Barbies look hot. We might have gotten into our mothers' make-up and played dress-up.

But somewhere around age 12, we girls start focusing on attracting more than a Ken doll. We start looking at the fashion magazines and the cosmetic ads. We go from not worrying too much about their looks to focusing on nothing but.

Beautiful girls can't see their own beauty. Girls with curls iron their hair. Girls with straight hair, at least when I was a teen, permed it.

Whatever we had needed to be different. And then we would be worthy of being loved and adored.

There have been commercials and videos documenting this. In one, women describe their looks to a police sketch artist, and then others describe them to the same artist. The sketches show beautiful women and completely inaccurate versions of them, depending on whom the artist was talking to at the time pencil was hitting paper.

Then another one showed women reacting to the things they themselves had said about their weight when those messages were put on posters and price tags in a fake dress shop. "Cellulite is in my DNA" and "#cow."

Why do we do this, ladies?

We'd never say such things about another person, say, a stranger on the street, and we'd be fighting mad if someone said those things about our daughters or our best friends. Why, then, do we do it to ourselves?

Why are we ugly to the beautiful woman in the mirror? Why can't we show her some love and accept her for who she is?

You know what's really hot? A woman who loves the skin she's in.

Confidence is the most attractive thing you can put on. Wear it well.

Your girls

If I could go back to my younger self, I would tell her this: Spend more time with your female friends and less with boys/men.

Little girls spend loads of time with each other growing up. Friendships are everything. We laughed together, played together, dreamed together and cried together.

And then girls grow up to get twitterpated.

Girls discover boys, and then the boyfriends can take precedence over just about everything—brain cells, reason, logic and, yes, your girls.

Then boyfriends become husbands, and then come children. And you wind up with bills to pay and chores to do. And they all tend to come before female friends, which is not a good thing.

Letting life's responsibilities crowd out time with female friends is a short-sighted thing.

Boyfriends leave.

Husbands either become ex-husbands or late husbands.

Children grow up and move away.

But your female friends?

Your girls are forever.

Seriously, if you don't go spend some time with your girls, who is going to hang out with you after you're no longer married and your children are in college?

Who's going to drink Margaritas with you or eat Ben & Jerry's?

Who's going to tell you you look skinny in the pants you know deep down make you look fat?

Who's going to tell you that the guy who left you was an idiot?

We tell a mix of truth and kind-hearted lies, and we affirm the hell out of each other, which is what BFFs are there for.

We'll also tell each other we're being stupid, but only after a glass of wine or two. And we try not to say "I told you so."

If we do, we say "I told her so" to mutual friends—we get the satisfaction of a good "I told you so" without the confrontation.

As I write, I am listening to a gaggle of tween-age girls in my living room, talking about what movie stars they think are cute, eating cinnamon rolls and braiding each other's hair. They had a sleepover party last night, which is an oxymoron. No sleep ever happens at those things. Just lots of hairstyling and laughing.

At their age, it is only about the friends. That's what makes their world go around.

But when we girls grow up into women, we make time for everyone and everything else. Except ourselves.

Jobs, relationships, children, church, keeping the house from looking like a train wreck. You name it.

But because time with friends is something we do for ourselves, we tend to push it to the back burner. And that is a shame, because if we did a few things for ourselves, just for the joy of it, we'd all be so much nicer to be around.

And who wouldn't appreciate a nicer mama, significant other, coworker or friend?

If I neglect being nice to myself, I notice I can be kind of a buzz kill. I lapse into Little Miss Perfect mode, doing everything I can think of at work and for family. That is followed by Little Miss Take You On A Guilt Trip. Yeah, those two paired up are loads of fun.

But get me together with some female friends over dinner, wine or just out walking on some nature trails, and I recharge.

It's better than "me" time, It's "us" time, and the love, acceptance and knowing our friends have been there and done that when we're going there and doing that fuels me up. It makes me stronger to have women I cheer on and who are in my amen corner in return.

Even when we're not together—and we aren't always as jobs and families have some of us scattered—we're like the stars. You know they're there, even if you don't see them all the time.

And when you do see them, it's like being twelve all over again. Only with less hair braiding and more laughter.

Catch and release

A male friend of mine tells the story of how a friend of his was saying, "There's other fish in the sea," quite frequently. He'd meet a woman, they'd date a few times, and then he'd move along.

"He's not fishing to take home a fish," he said. "He's using the catch and release method."

There are men and women who are on the catch and release plan. Because it is just so much fun to catch a fish, but they have no idea what to do with it once it is in the boat. Casting a line and reeling something in is great fun. Who knows what's going to be on the other end of that fishing line? Could be a whale. Or a rubber boot. Who knows?

But then it is a normal fish.

Like B.B. King sings, the thrill is gone.

If you've ever been fishing, you know it is a messy business. And I don't even bait my own hooks. And hooks, by the way, can get stuck everywhere. I got poked in the thumb by one, and it is not pleasant. Neither is dating by the catch and release method.

Now since I am not an expert fisherwoman, I went online to see what information was out there. It turns out that the Pennsylvania Fish & Boat Commission has information on their website about catching and releasing. You can take this to be about fishing, or you can take this to be about dating. Which aren't that different.

Every angler should expect and be prepared to release some portion of his catch, the website says. If you are dating instead of baiting, you might have to release just about all of them, depending on where you cast your line and who bites.

- ✓ The number of fish who survive depends on where the fish is hooked, the length of the fight and how the fish is handled and released.
- ✓ No barbs on the hooks. Otherwise, both the angler and the fish could get hurt.
- ✓ Try to land your fish as quickly as possible, but don't play the fish to exhaustion. Exhausted fish can be short on patience and long on bad attitudes.
- ✓ You don't want your fish to be out of water long. This is so true, because I just hate feeling like a fish out of water. Staying in familiar waters is good for all concerned.
- ✓ Watch out for the chance of bacterial infection. Enough said.
- ✓ Remove hooks quickly, but if you can't do this without harming the fish, cut the lines. It's amazing how many fishermen never cut their lines. They throw back a fish and then blow up the fish's cell phone after too many Budweisers. Research has documented that cutting the line can greatly increase the survival of deeply hooked fish, the Pennsylvania Fish & Boat Commission experts write. So just cut the lines, people.
- ✓ Allow the fish to swim away under its own power. And once you have let go of the fish, don't go chasing after it, pleading, "Baby, I've changed! Give me a second chance." Because the fish will laugh at you.

There's the saying that there are other fish in the sea. Once the metaphorical fish swims off, someone invariably tells the angler that there are other fish in the sea. Anglers who use the catch and release method know this already.

The late comedian Patrice O'Neal had a routine based on fishing. He compared men throwing out their lines, so to speak, with the reason why some men want to have a boat.

Why?

"To prove I can still catch fish," he said.

I think this may have a lot to do with why some date with the catch and release method. They want to prove that someone is still going to chomp down on their bait for a chance at getting reeled into the boat.

Otherwise, they don't want the fish.

And the poor fish find out that they are out of their element.

The moral of this fish tale is that fish need to swim fast and be particular about what hook and line they plan to swallow.

Wildebeests

One of my single girlfriends posted something about her singleness on Facebook. Like we all do from time to time.

And then one of her male friends decided to give us women some advice.

Or a lecture. And you know how well that works, right?

I am paraphrasing, but his post on the thread went something like this: "You can't find a good man because you are so used to the bad ones that when you do stumble upon a good man, you look at him as if you have found a wildebeest. And if you decided to take the wildebeest home, you wouldn't have the slightest idea what to do with it."

That was harsh. And pretty funny.

So I decided that I needed to read up on wildebeests if I was ever going to bring one home. And here is what I found online. It turns out wildebeests and some men may not be so different after all.

- ✓ Wildebeests look like a cross between a moose and a bull.
- ✓ They have skinny legs but rather large noggins.
- ✓ Wildebeests are roaming around day and night. They are constantly on the move.
- ✓ During mating season, small groups form within herds. Five or six male wildebeests in these groups stake out territory that females wander through. Sound familiar?
- ✓ The shenanigans of the territorial bulls while the lady wildebeests are around got them the name "clowns of the savanna." I think I have met

some of their human counterparts, "clowns of the sports bar."

- ✓ When these bull wildebeests meet at the edges of their territories, they snort and fight. They proceed to butt heads. If you want to think about them as "buttheads," go right ahead.
- ✓ Nonterritorial bull wildebeests travel in "bachelor herds." I have spotted these in human form as well.
- ✓ If disturbed, according to the website outofafrica.nl, male wildebeests "snort explosively."

Explosive snorting aside, the idea of bringing home a wildebeest is intriguing. My male friends say that women really don't want good men or nice guys. Chicks dig the bad boys, they say. And for some of us, that is true. It has to be, otherwise the sales of Ben & Jerry's would plummet and there would be a lot more lonely men.

But when you grow up, you realize that a bad boy will only become a man with substance abuse issues. You realize that you're a good woman and you realize that you're worth more and deserve more.

Then, and only then, should you go looking in the savanna for the elusive wildebeest.

As for a wildebeest's care and feeding, they thrive on tender, loving care and seem to be fond of beer, nachos, ice cream and anything off the grill.

Men who can't spell

"I will give my heart and sole to you."
"Your great."
"Your welcome."
Laughing yet?

There are lots more of these spelling and grammar faux pas out there. I don't know if it's the men perpetrating these screw-ups or just that I see them from men more, but, Lord, have mercy.

Did you boys sleep during English class?

This might make you wake up, then.

Now that men and women seem to be meeting more on dating websites and social media, your command of your mother tongue will either make you or break you romantically.

We women will judge you on your grammar. I do.

I have laughed out loud at some Facebook messages and emails, and have even told friends about them. Now, given that I work as an editor during some of my day and that one of my besties is an English teacher, we may be the grammar police.

I have never been rude to someone about their grammar and spelling and the like when they've approached me electronically.

But just know that every comma splice and misuse of vocabulary is like a giant piece of spinach on your front teeth, men. It is the typed equivalent of having your fly unzipped. It just makes a horrible first impression.

Back in the day, when men and women would talk, spelling errors weren't so obvious because people don't have those cartoon quote bubbles over their heads. And thank the Lord they don't have those cartoon thought bubbles floating around up top. That would be too much information for everyone.

Unless you have a ridiculously good-looking photo of yourself, an incoherent, misspelled profile on a dating website will only get you women who think incoherent and misspelled is normal.

And don't forget your punctuation. "I enjoy cooking, my family and pets," reads like you are a nice person. "I enjoy cooking my family and pets," reads like you are a psychopath. Commas save lives, including your love life.

I do realize there are people out there who are just not good with words. And I get that, because I am not good with numbers. There are people out there who don't know the difference between its and it's who would laugh at me struggling to balance a checkbook, but here's the deal.

Life is not fair. You could put compute pi to 30 places to the right of the decimal, but it's not going to tell the rest of the dating world whether you like Italian food and if your favorite color is blue.

Sooner or later, you're going to have to communicate with words on a screen.

If not when you begin dating, it will be when you are dating and you need to send a text.

And there's a whole different language for that. IKR? (I know, right?)

TTYL. BRB. LOL. And one we've giggled about – K.

Just K. Shortened from "OK." Because it takes a lot of effort to type in that O.

One of the Dear Sons and I have laughed over the meaning of this little acronym. WTF.

It is much nicer to read as an acronym, by the way.

We decided it should mean, "Well, that's fantastic."

When he texted me he had a 4.0 average, I texted back, "WTF."

I can only do that with the Dear Son, though. Not everyone gets our jokes.

And there comes a time when the acronyms don't save time. Because sometimes you have to respond by explaining them. In which you would have just said what you meant to say when you typed in the alphabet soup.

Then there are Facebook messages. I happen to like Facebook's message feature, as it is faster than email in the newsroom. Plus, there are sources of mine who don't always answer their cell phones or respond to emails, but they always—always—reply to a Facebook message.

Relationshipwise, though, Facebook is a minefield. If you are borderline illiterate, it will show.

Plus there is the whole issue of relationship status. Having been shell-shocked by this a few times, I am not changing my relationship status again until I am legally married.

Even then, I think the ink should be dry on the marriage license before I click on anything.

These days, you're not really married until you change that Facebook relationship status.

Then there are the folks who want to read all your Facebook postings. These are either stalkers or your significant other, who, in this case, is also a stalker.

All this is enough to make a single person do something drastic.

Like talk to someone face to face.

Purse holders

I see them all the time.

Purseholders.

These men, having lost all sense of manhood and hope, are left sitting on park benches at art shows, flea markets and outlet malls, holding their wives' purses.

And sometimes worse.

I once was looking at photos one of the newspaper photographers came back from the Canton Flea Market, and there he was: A husband holding his wife's purse.

But it only got worse.

Strapped to his chest like a baby was a rat-sized foo-foo dog, probably one of those designer breeds ending in "poo," "tzu" or "doodle."

If there is one thing worse for a man's manhood than being a purseholder, it is being a rat-sized dog holder. Why not just dress the man up in a pink tutu?

Married women, I blame you for this.

No man turns himself into a purseholder.

No, he gets forced into it.

Women, you see these perfectly manly men, go fall in love with one of them for his manly qualities, and then, once the ring is on, you start handing him your purse.

Not all men will take to being a purseholder. Back in the days when I was married to my late husband who I'll call Baby Daddy, if I would have handed him my purse, he'd have let it drop and left it where it fell, so I knew better.

But I see the men who are purseholders, and I feel badly for them.

There have been days when, as a single, I would question why I was alone with no one to hand my purse to, if I had chosen to. However, I knew that my purse was best left on my own shoulder.

This does beg the question of why married women have purseholders they're taking for granted?

Loneliness will make you ask God crazy questions like this.

God, I believe, does have a sense of humor. He keeps it next door to his sense of irony. Why else would women who don't believe in turning men into purseholders not have men, when women who do hand off their purses and rat-sized dogs do? That is a question for the ages.

Anyhow, the worst I will do is ask my Gentleman Friend to watch my purse if I am stepping away from the restaurant table, being careful to leave the bag in my seat and not too terribly close to him.

Ladies, hate me if you must, but there ought to be something in the wedding vows about letting men look manly and not making them carry handbags that clearly don't go with their outfits.

"Do you promise to love, honor and not make your man look girly by making him carry a Kate Spade clutch and wear a rat-sized dog strapped to his chest? In sickness and in health, for richer, for poorer, even when you are at the mall and your hands are full?"

Something along those lines.

Because men really do hate holding handbags. If I didn't learn anything else the first time Baby Daddy didn't tote my purse, I learned that.

My theory on the purseholder phenomenon is that holding a purse makes a man look taken. As in way more than wearing a wedding band would.

A ball and chain wouldn't make him look any less available.

And while purse-handing women love the manly traits their future hubbies had before they wed, turning the spouse into a purseholder accomplishes two things. It makes the Mr. look super taken, to the point of no return taken, and it frees up your hands because you no longer have to tote your tote.

We women are all about multitasking.

The horrors of marriage

Maybe this is the result of too many men being forced into purse holding.

Maybe it has to do with carrying enough baggage from failed relationships to fill a U-Haul.

Or maybe it is all the ball-and-chain stereotypes about marriage that are believed because, well, like most stereotypes, there is a grain of truth to them.

Whatever the reason, there are quite a few men in their 40s and 50s who are horrified at the idea of being married again if they were married before or at the thought of being married at all.

I don't get this, because men have traditionally come out pretty well in marriage over the decades. They've gotten clean houses and hot meals, plus the whole being king of the castle thing.

When I was growing up, you'd wonder if men had a clue how to pour a glass of iced tea or fix a plate, because they did neither. Ever.

But apparently the first wives of today's world have managed to wreck a few now-divorced men out there, because the thought of anything involving a preacher, rings, eating a holiday dinner together, being in a relationship, committing to a date or admitting you "like like" someone scares the bejeezus out of some men.

And their single friends, too.

Married women, you may want to pause now and thank Jesus for your hubby and go cook a roast and some mashed potatoes.

Because the single life of the fortysomething woman is filled with men who are petrified at the thought of commitment. I know, because on more than one occasion, the thought of dating me long enough for commitment to be a consideration has scared off a man. Apparently actually being married to me would be sheer hell.

But I digress.

Let's talk about the single men out there. The never-been-marrieds. If a man reaches four decades and isn't married, there's a darned good reason for it.

Maybe he hoards action figures and comic books or plays Dungeons and Dragons-type card games obsessively.

Or he's a player who can't quit the game, and in this case, the game is not Magic The Gathering or D&D.

Maybe he grew up around enough bad marriages to make him want to live in a cave.

Who knows? But trust me, there is a reason that no one has decided to be Mrs. Cave-dweller or Mrs. Player or Mrs. Magic The Gathering. Which is fine, because they're pretty happy as they are.

Then there are the divorced guys.

They live in fear of the rest of the world's women being just like the first wife.

And she may not have been so bad, given that there is always another side to everyone's story.

Maybe she wasn't as crazy as he makes her out to be unless crazy means she was tired of putting up with his shenanigans.

Anyhow, there's this saying out there that women over forty have a better chance of being killed by terrorists than marrying, so I looked it up to see if it was truth or urban myth.

Snopes.com says that's not true.

Unless you meet some of these men, and then, yes, the terrorists may have a good chance of winning after all.

Honestly, I don't understand men. I have heard men on multiple occasions criticize the act of being "too nice" and offering them food.

One male friend was acting all girlie about his girlfriend leaving food for him in his refrigerator.

By girlie I mean that he was overthinking everything, which is what we women do. A lot.

"What do you think she meant by that?" he asked. "Do you think she is trying to move in? She's wanting to get too serious."

"I think she wanted to give you something to eat," I said, trying not to be rudely obvious with my eye-rolling.

Apparently diamonds don't mean engagement to men, but a home-cooked meal does.

Some men hate kind words. How devious of us, plying them with fried chicken and verbal sweetness. These men are happy as they are or they wouldn't keep doing what they do. I wish them well and hope they find the unkind women of their dreams.

Women who have their lives and jobs under control, who are good people raising terrific kids and furthering themselves professionally ... we're as close to man repellant as cats.

At least to some men.

Being married to us would be, well, horrifying. At least to them.

Can you imagine the horrors of being committed to a woman who has her act together?

This part of the dating experience, for me as well as other women I know, has been alternately insulting and just plain ridiculous at times.

Insulting because some men think being married to us would be a fate worse than death, and ridiculous because so many of them think women are so jumping-up-and-down eager to be their Mrs. that any act of kindness toward them is seen as trying to drag them down the first aisle we come across.

Men who complain they never can find a nice girl to date, this is why. You assume that the nice ones are trying to make you purseholders, so you run them off.

I may get killed by terrorists for saying this, but I'm pretty happy these days with my single self.

If it was legal in the state of Mississippi, I would marry myself. And I'd be one lucky girl, because I am a heck of a catch.

I've got other single women friends in the same boat, only they consider that boat of singleness to be a luxury yacht. They love living on their own and don't consider themselves to be alone.

Because, well, they're not.

They have all kinds of friends and their beautiful children and jobs they love. They run and paint and sing and dance away their free time. In short, they liver rich, full lives.

Life is good, and they're not putting anything on hold waiting for a man to overcome his mountains of fear to pop something resembling a question.

It's taken me years of midlife dating to see this, but it is all about being happy where you are and with who you are.

Who you are with, as it turns out, shouldn't define your happiness or lack thereof.

Be happy being yourself and being with yourself.

Ladies, we haven't lived this long without learning to be pretty fantastic along the way, and by now, some man's fear of commitment shouldn't be the difference between loving life and not.

Let's continue being the great moms and power women and dear friends, roles that define our lives. Let's be kind to ourselves instead of horrifying commitment-shy men with good deeds that go unappreciated.

Let's continue being great catches, whether there are fishermen around or not.

Wasbands

Sometimes you come upon a term that is sheer perfection. It is not original to me, although I wish it was because it is just that darned clever. One of my BIFFLS—or Best Friends For Life—came up with it.

She calls her ex-husband a "wasband."

As in "was" and not "is."

Some of my friends have several wasbands, and some of my male friends are wasbands.

Since my own personal wasband went to his great reward nearly a decade ago, I don't have a whole lot of experience relating to wasbands.

But my friends' wasbands are, for the most part, alive and well, and they get along just fine with them. Some of my divorced friends get along better with their ex-husbands as wasbands than they ever did when their wasbands were husbands.

They'll talk about how their wasbands came over to fix things or take the kids off their hands or mow the yard or whatever, and they'll talk about how they're wonderful but thank God they aren't married to them anymore.

I've said on more than one occasion, "If you're not using him, can I borrow him sometime?"

Because it's not like Baby Daddy is coming back, and I have chores on the to-do list.

I think the beauty of having a living wasband is that you can get them to do things for you without having to do much or anything in return. At least, that's how my friends put it. No wifely duties but they get the house painted.

Some of the wasbands I know really take issue, though, when their exes call themselves single parents.

One friend of mine's ex-wife was entered in a contest for Mother's Day. While she didn't mail the entry, he said she did have a hand in writing it. It went on about her struggling as a single parent, and my friend said, "The checks were coming every month and I was there helping."

His exact words were something to the effect of, "Single, my ass."

My thought here is that nobody is more of a single parent than a widow or a widower and the never-been-married folks. True single parents have zero back-up.

Some days I have thought it might be handy to go marry someone and then divorce him just so I could have a wasband with some home repair skills.

Before I started dating again, I would say, "If Bob Vila would show up on my doorstep, I would marry him. And then put him to work."

Or divorce him, because I could see him having good wasband potential.

Honestly, though, I have wondered about those with wasbands who they get along with. I even know several wasbands who still help home school their children.

If you can get along with a wasband well enough for you two, as a united front, to teach your children algebra, then why in the world did you get divorced?

I was married for 18 years, and I can tell you that many times we didn't get along nearly as well as some ex-wives and wasbands I know do. Our children would have been about as smart as a box of rocks if we had ever tried to home school them.

Marriage is not a rose garden, you know. It's not by accident that the "for better or for worse" part is in the vows, because, trust me, there will be a "for worse."

So if you can't get through the "for worse" part, how is it that you can get through the "we're divorced" part?

My theory on this is that some divorced couples get along well because they know, in their heart of hearts, that they don't have to go home together at the end of the day. They can put up with each other for an hour to be good parents at the school play because they know there is an end to the evening.

But with marriage, they know there is no end. The vows have that "As long as you both shall live" part in there.

The same person you saw at night will be the same one you see in the morning, only with bad hair and worse breath.

And exes and wasbands tend to be less possessive and less bossy than they were when they were legally wedded.

Maybe more marriages would last if couples got along as well and gave each other as much space as some ex-wives and wasbands give each other.

Doing nothing

Doing a bunch of nothing is actually something.

That's become my standard of excellence in relationships. It took quite a few years for me to figure that out, so learn from this hard-earned wisdom.

Many women believe that dating and time with friends is all about what you are doing and where you are going. It is about seeing and being seen.

But really, when you are with true friends and your true love, nothing's a pretty good thing to be doing. Because if you can do nothing with someone happily, then you can do anything with them. And that's something.

When you are 20 and dating, you are always doing something. Because that is what twentysomethings do. Twentysomethings are something waiting for a place to happen.

But when you go back to the dating world in your forties, or find yourself for the first time in a decade or more with the luxury of having time for your girlfriends, you find out quickly that you can't do nothing with just anyone.

It's a special person you can be with when the only activity is just being and not also doing.

There are some people you will come across in life who are fun if you are doing something fun together. There are those you have to have a plan in order to be with. An agenda. A travel plan and Julie the cruise director to line up a game of shuffleboard.

Because otherwise, you would have to just look at each other and breathe the same air.

And if you weren't doing something together or watching something you could discuss later, what on earth would you talk about?

And I will tell you that it is never a good sign if you have to drink to be around someone. One should never hang out with someone you need to drink to stand. If their personality is in your bottle of wine, then alcoholism could be in your future.

I once knew that a relationship was doomed when there was a two Bud Light minimum for us to be in the same room.

But those women you can go walking with and after a few hours, you're wondering where the time went, and a man who doing nothing with can be preferable to doing something or going somewhere, those are the people you let into your heart.

It's those people who can be themselves around you, and you don't care. And you can be yourself around them, and they love you anyway.

You never have to worry about what to say or if there will be a lull in the conversation because there never is.

When you're with them, you don't worry about the possibility of actually doing nothing because when you get together, you may start doing nothing but it turns into going somewhere or doing something that will turn into a great story later.

A story that you can tell each other the next time you're doing nothing on the way to doing something.

Men worth having

Never settle for being with anyone less than a man worth having.

The alternative, after all, is being with a Man Not Worth Having, and those aren't worth having. Those are the ones you beg your girlfriends not to date, keep your mouth shut about while they're dating them anyway and then tell your girlfriends that these men are idiots when the inevitable break-up happens.

And you know that the break-up will happen because they're not called Men Not Worth Having for nothing.

They will take what promises to be a great relationship and screw it up on purpose and then blame it all on you.

If you were a better woman, their reasoning goes, they'd have never strayed.

Your wants and wishes don't really matter to them. Unless, of course, your wants and wishes happen to be something they, too, want and wish for. Duh.

Now if only you could wish for beer, NASCAR and chasing women.

Their behavior is never their fault, but always yours.

Then, when you're done with their shenanigans, because, after all, they are called Men Not Worth Having, at least by me, they make you feel like something's wrong with you and make you cry until Ben and Jerry's helps you make it through the night.

Then, just when you are over him, he blows up your phone begging for a second chance.

But a Man Worth Having. That's who to have.

If you find yourself with one of those, thank Jesus for him every night. Go out of your way to be sweet to him, and never, ever take him for granted.

They're quite rare and should be treated as such.

A Man Worth Having is one you can count on. If he's late, you know there was a line at the Kroger or traffic or an act of God and not just another round at the local pub. He keeps his word, and his name's something to live up to, not something to live down.

He's not into making you jealous by the way he looks at other women.

Instead, he leaves other women jealous of you just by the way he treats you. Who wouldn't want to be you?

A Man Worth Having isn't scared away by your kids or your cats.

He knows life can fall apart some days, but he'll come over and help you pick up the pieces and glue them back together.

He knows you have baggage, but he'll help you unpack.

Everyone is reliable, even if what's reliable about them is their unreliability. A Man Worth Having is reliably reliable.

He saves drama for date nights to the movies.

He will tell you you're beautiful when you're having a bad hair day and there's not a drop of makeup on your face.

A Man Worth Having is who you want your sons to grow up to be like.

Forcing roses

Our house in West Point, the one I grew up in, had the floral evidence of my mother and grandmother. Rose bushes dotted the landscape here and there. Soft pink ones on the side of the house, and a pinkish red variety up the stairs leading to the back door.

I loved them. As a little girl, I would rejoice over the buds.

But my complete lack of patience would get the best of me. I couldn't stand the wait from bud to blossom.

I would take hold of a perfectly good rosebud and start peeling back the tightly wound little petals.

Of course, what I wound up with was not a full and beautifully blossomed rose.

Instead, I had a pile of torn-up rosebuds.

There was a time that we didn't have that many blossoms due to my attempts to hatch roses before their time.

Like Tom Petty sings, "The waiting is the hardest part."

Also the not knowing.

Because something happens to us single fortysomethings. We realize that there's not as much daylight to burn as there was a few years ago.

Every day I look a little bit more like my mother, and I don't mean as a younger woman.

Lines that were not on my face yesterday will be there tomorrow.

I can truthfully say the color of my hair is mine because I bought it myself.

For the first time in our lives, we question how many good years we have left. And what are the chances that we, in our dwindling years, are going to find love?

We get this feeling that there is not a moment to waste when it comes to dating.

As one of my female friends put it, "I've got one foot in the grave."

If you've only got one foot above ground, are you going to waste that good foot on a bad relationship, or just dating to avoid boredom?

At this age, if you know you are not with your dream man, you tend to bolt for the nearest door or window.

In other words, if you can't imagine one day being married to this person, or at least happily dating in a committed, loving relationship, then by your forties, you want to cut bait and start fishing elsewhere.

If one of your feet is six feet under, you don't want to spend a second longer on something that ends in anything short of what you want.

I can't tell you the times I have personally wished for a crystal ball. Not one of those Magic 8 Balls, but one that tells the unadulterated truth about the present and future.

If I had one of these crystal balls each time I wished for one, and one that is in good working order, I would have asked for winning lottery numbers, the best funds in which to park my 401(k) and where my relationship at the time was going.

Because if said relationship is going to be a disaster of Biblical proportions in the near future, then I need to find something more productive to do with my time than try to make something work that won't work. If it's not going to work at the end, then time's a-wastin'.

My good years, the ones before I start forgetting things and begin growing a neck wattle, are, as the soap opera said, "like sands through the hour glass."

So, with the days of our lives frittering away, if I have what appears to be a perfectly good rosebud of a relationship, my impatience wants to start dissecting it, figuring out where it's going and what makes it work.

The only thing is, when you start peeling off rose petals, it kills the rose. When you start tinkering around with relationships to see what makes them work, those relationships stop working.

As hard as it may be to do, waiting is what has to happen to see if and when a relationship is going to grow, and if it does, what it's going to grow into.

Roses are better than kudzu or poison sumac.

As difficult as it may be, ladies, we have to give these things some time. If a rose is growing into a rose, it's not going to grow like chia seeds. Rush things, and you get a big old Chia pet.

Take the time with what appears to be a perfectly good rose to be and see if that is what it turns into.

If it's true and we really don't have a pile of good years left, then let's spend them on letting something blossom.

As one of my Match.com friends, a man I chatted with but never met in person, told me, "If it is meant to be, you can't stop it from happening. If it is not meant to be, nothing you can do will bring it to pass."

No matter how bad you think your gardening skills are, give something that looks like a good thing time to prove itself. One day, when you least expect it, after waiting, weeding, watering and maybe some Miracle-Gro and prayer, you'll have a rose on your hands.

The right one

We women used to be little girls, and little girls listen to fairy tales.

Lots and lots of fairy tales.

One of the things that women learn from the time they are knee-high to June bugs is that there is "the one" out there.

That one true love who will come rescue you. Then you're a short carriage ride away to happily ever after.

Many times, over many bad hair days and nothing to wear days, I have wished for a Fairy Godmother, but alas. I haven't had one show up so far.

We're adults now, though, and we realize that fairy tales are not real.

Still, the idea of "the one" being out there persists.

I like to believe he's out there.

Or lots of Prince Charmings, one for every woman.

My mama had her Prince Charming.

Her Prince Charming was my daddy, and while he wasn't the most smooth-around-the-edges man you'd ever meet and very nearly drove my mama crazy on a few occasions, he was "the one" for her.

He knew it, she knew it and so did everyone else.

The fairy tale heroines had it a little easier than we real-life women in that they could tell who their prince was. He was the one who kissed her out of a witch-induced coma. Duh.

The rest of us have to hunt our princes.

With this in mind, here are a few princely qualities you might want to keep an eye out for. Watch for these traits, and you can tell the princes from the frogs.

- Princes will claim you as their princess instead of taking great pains to look available.
- Princes never disrespect you.
- Princes do come to your rescue. The rescue might involve fixing a dishwasher or a broken pipe rather than slaying a dragon, but a rescue's a rescue.
- Princes are also awesome at protecting you. That's what they do. They would never knowingly put you in a dangerous situation.
- The one for you knows the difference between claiming you and being possessive. He can share you with family and friends and doesn't feel threatened when you go out to dinner on a ladies' night out.

- Princes want you to succeed. Your wins are a win for them, too.
- Princes know that you can do it all, but they'd never let you do it all or make you do it all.
- Princes know romance. They know how to cook candlelit dinners including herbs and veggies they grew themselves, but they also know there is nothing more romantic than a man who washes dishes.
- Princes expect princesses. They want you to be one and that brings out the best in you. Ladies, make sure you conduct yourselves in a princess-like manner.
- Once a prince has his princess, he knows better than to treat her as anything less than one.

The kids

It is one of the negatives of working in the news business. Every so often you come across a story about some woman who puts up with God knows what kind of abuse being done to her, her children, her finances or her car at the hands of a boyfriend.

Why does she stay? And why would she put up with harm being done to her sweet babies, who she was put on this earth to look out for?

Invariably, the answer to that question is, "Because I love him."

And at that moment, my head explodes.

"Why?" you ask. What is lovable about someone who shows cruelty to you or your children or disrespects you and your loved ones?

I am not saying this never happens the other way around, with men letting their brains fall out of their heads over women who are awful to them and any children in the picture. Unfortunately, it does.

But some women, the ones who fear being alone more than they fear their babies or their checking accounts, housing or cars being hurt, will stay with Mr. Awful.

This ought to be one of those self-evident truths like the ones in the Declaration of Independence, but apparently it needs stating.

So here it is: Men come and go, but your children are FOREVER.

Children are precious gifts, and when you get one, it is God's way of saying, "Don't screw this up. Your job is now to protect and raise this little child until he or she is old enough to go out on his or her own. Period."

So with this in mind, when I began to date after my late husband's passing, I decided that the kids needed to stay numero uno in my list of priorities.

They are like the U.S. and Russia on the United Nations Security Council: Veto Powers.

They don't like someone I am seeing? Well, then, throw some butter and jelly on him because that fellow is toast.

I know some single moms and dads who hold off on introducing their sort-of-significant other to their children.

Their logic is that they don't want to introduce their children to who they are dating until things are fairly serious.

To each her own or his own, but to me, the horse has already left the stable by that point.

If your children can't stand the person you are dating but you are head over heels for them, then things will get messy in a hurry. Those are the situations soap operas, counseling sessions and crime reports are made of.

No, I believe in letting my children know who I spend my time with right off the bat.

My Gentleman Friend got to meet my sweet babies, or at least a couple of them, on our first date.

The reason he is still my Gentleman Friend is because the kids like him. I am rather fond of him, too, but if the kids would have given him a thumbs-down, I don't think there would have been a second date.

Letting your kids check out your dates early in the game means that you won't become emotionally twitterpated with someone who will not pass muster with your kiddos.

Few people know you as well as your youngsters.

And few people want the best for you like your children do.

Letting them say yea or nay to who you spend your time with can give you insight you wouldn't otherwise have. Because, if you are emotionally twitterpated, then you're not completely in your right mind.

At best, you're not quite objective. At worst, you are too stupid to be walking around on your own.

Insight, at this juncture, is something you need as much as oxygen. So breathe it in.

Listen to what they have to say. Not only for their good intentions for their mama, but also for the fact that kids and dogs tend to like good people. God help the man who your children and your dog hate.

Remarriages, statisticians say, are more likely than first marriages to end with a divorce.

Why not give the second time around a better chance by letting your children have a say? If you know, from the get-go, that your beau is roundly despised by your children, then (a) why is he your beau and (b) why would you go into this thinking that it would work?

And if you say, "But I LOVE him," then realize you have made my case for giving an intro to your kids before anyone uses the L word.

Multiple single parent friends of mine have been distressed over their special friends not being all ga-ga over their kids. Understand that few people are going to love your sweet babies as much as you do, but if you are going to be in a committed relationship with someone, and you have children, they need to be a close second to you when it comes to the love and welfare of your children.

And if you are dating someone who begrudges time that you spend with your children and can't understand why you have to put your children first, then ask yourself why you are dating this person. It's a rhetorical question.

Whether you are a parent or not, your significant other should want your life to be as rich and full as possible. If you are a parent, that life has to including not only raising but enjoying your children, who, again, are FOREVER.

Don't negotiate on the non-negotiables.

If your children say no, if your prospective significant other can't understand why your children have to come first, if he isn't secure enough to encourage you to enjoy your children, knowing that you will think he's even more of a prince for it, then, in the words of one of my besties, a fellow single mama, "Next!"

Marriage

My mama and daddy used to talk about *knowing*, knowing like they knew the sun was going to come up, that they were marrying the right person.

At least that is what they'd say.

I was married once, to my late husband Baby Daddy, and I wanted to believe he was the right person, that one man on the planet I was meant to spend the rest of my life beside. Like, if we were in a Disney movie, we'd be singing to each other.

I wanted to know like mama and daddy knew, like Cinderella and Prince Charming knew.

But I didn't. Instead, the week of our wedding, I was having panic attacks and cold sweats.

I knew, alright. I knew I was terrified.

Which, looking back, is exactly how I should have felt.

Not to call my parents liars, but I think they may have been stretching the truth or dipping it in candy coating.

I know that you can't *know*.

You can't know you're agreeing to live out your days with the person that God put on the planet just for you, the one ordained to alternately drive you up a wall or make you smile on a regular basis.

For better or for worse, for richer, for poorer. You can't know that it will all be better and richer. Instead, it's a fairly safe bet there will be worse and poorer mixed in there.

You can't know you won't grow apart. One or both of you may change and probably will.

You can't even know that the person you think you are marrying is the person you, in fact, are marrying. People have been known to be on their best behavior during courtship, saving all manner of gas-passing until after the "I dos" are said.

You can think they are the one, or be pretty sure.

But you can't *know*.

Instead, you can do what my mama and daddy actually did, if they were telling the truth, and what countless couples have done.

They didn't know they had entered holy matrimony with the one person right for them. Instead, they *decided* that they were with their soul mate.

Every blessed day they made that decision.

Maybe every hour. It's just like a 12-Step program. Count the time how it suits you. Make that decision accordingly and as needed.

Deciding is active but not always easy. Usually, it's not.

These couples choose to love and honor even when they didn't feel like loving or honoring and even when their spouses are not being particularly lovable or honorable.

When I knew I was married, when I was going to have to decide to know this was the one, was during our first argument.

I wanted to leave.

But I couldn't because I realized that if I did, I was leaving my home.

So I did what all dedicated wives do. I stayed and fought.

I didn't stay because I knew I was with the man for me. I stayed because I decided he was and that hanging in there matrimony-wise was worth doing even when I didn't particularly feel like it.

About half of marriages end in divorce, and some marriages may not be safe or healthy. Some of them need to end.

Some of those brides and grooms, though, think they know. Right up until they don't. Until the make-up is off and the kids are sick and he's lost his job. Until knowing that's who you are supposed to spend your days alongside is a horrifying thought.

It's a choice to act as if the one you pledged your love to is your happiness, because they probably won't be on an everyday basis.

It's easy to be in love when it's all wedding cake and better and richer. When worse and poorer hit is when you make the "I do" decision daily.

Rules of engagement

When did getting engaged turn into the equivalent of winning a game show?

You outshine the other ladies in the Plinko game of dating. He's in L-O-V-E and, as Beyonce sings, liked it enough to attempt to put a ring on it.

Call it bling-bling gone cray-cray.

Engage-a-palooza.

A normal man, according to Bride magazine, spends about $5,000, on average on a diamond for his beloved. And again, this is on average. Some men spend a lot more, and some head to the jewelry counter at Wal-Mart.

Celebrity men, though. Normal men should despise them. They're like the guy down the street who makes all the other men look bad by being the uber husband and spoiling his wife to the point that you wonder what he's done wrong that he has to make up for.

With the whopper diamonds celebrity men have been putting on the ring fingers of their celebrity girlfriends, you have to wonder if normal women are expecting bigger rocks than their mamas and grandmamas got.

Take this celebrity intelligence gleaned from all manner of supermarket tabloids into account:

Justin Timberlake planted an 18-carat ring on Jessica Biel's finger.

But NBA star Kris Humphries popped for a 20.5-carat diamond ring for Kim Kardashian. It cost him, allegedly, $2 million, although he might have gotten a deal. Since the marriage only lasted 72 days, I hope he did.

Still, $2 million. That is 20 times the amount of my mortgage, which was a crazy big, keep-you-up-at-night amount of money for me. I couldn't sleep the night before I signed off on that.

I think I got a better deal than Kris did, and I also think I sweated more over it.

Kanye West, though, went a little smaller than Kris: $1.5 million for a 15-carat diamond ring when he popped the question to Kim Kardashian once she was divorced from Kris. Oh, and that previous engagement ring? It was sold at auction for $620,000.

With rings the size of these, I am thinking celebrity fiancees must lift weights just to open a diet soda while wearing their engagement rings, but what am I thinking? They have people for that.

Used to be, dropping to one knee with a little velvet box from the jewelry store was enough for the popping of the question.

Now it has to be an event.

There are proposal messages towed through the clouds by airplanes, and symphony orchestras playing the prospective fiancee's favorite song. Since we're keeping up with the Kardashians, it's worth noting that Kanye West rented out a ballpark for $35,000 as a wedding proposal site. $35,000 sounds like chump change next to the price of the ring.

There are men who invite all the friends and family over for a big open-bar party to celebrate, which sounds a lot like a pre-wedding-reception wedding reception. When they go to all the trouble to throw a big party to celebrate, you just hope after all that work, she said yes.

Then there are the showers and more parties. Bachelorette and bachelor parties. Lingerie showers and round-the-clock hen parties where ladies bring a gift suitable for use at the hour they are assigned. Toasters for 7 a.m. Fondue pots for 8 o'clock at night.

Then there's the wedding and all the parties before, during and after.

It's all great fun, at least until the bills come in.

The fact is that a wedding can be had for less $100 or for millions. The only limit is your imagination and line of credit.

The paupers are just as married as the princes and princesses, except the frugal fiances aren't going to get hit with the stress, headaches and financial obligations.

They're the ones who have a big dose of reality with engagements and weddings that aren't beyond their means, and they're also less likely to set themselves up for money arguments since they're not starting out with their credit cards maxxed out with engagement hoopla and wedding expenses.

The couples who start out with their engagement and wedding to rival the royals are heading for a big letdown.

Married life, as it turns out, is nothing like engaged life. Engaged life is lots of shopping with a party or two every week. Married life means that someone has to cook dinner, a pipe just broke and the yard needs mowing.

A big diamond, a whoop-de-do proposal and a string of parties does not a marriage make.

When you've met the right one, the prize isn't the ring or the parties or the honeymoon dream vacation.

The prize is who you share your life with.

Choose wisely.

I can't wait no more

It was a usual day in Clay County Circuit Court.

Drug-related guilty pleas. A few property crime cases. A couple of folks with suspended sentences who got into trouble again and were getting sent to the county lock-up for the original misdeeds that started it all.

Same old stuff, I thought. I was working as a newspaper reporter in West Point, Mississippi, at the time, and wasn't seeing anything out of the ordinary in court that day.

But then I saw them.

A man in a dark suit, and, with him, a woman wearing a bridal gown and veil.

Not the normal courtroom attire.

They waited their turn before the bench patiently. Or as patiently as they could.

The circuit clerk came before the judge and, speaking softly, told the judge what this soon-to-be-married couple was doing in court instead of in church.

Then the judge, speaking at judge volume, told the rest of us the deal. This couple had thought of everything for their wedding except for one thing: getting a marriage license.

That was a problem, as this didn't occur to them until they were in a church full of their friends and relatives. The only thing to do, they figured, was to throw themselves on the mercy of the court.

In Mississippi, there is a three-day waiting period from the time you apply for a marriage license to the time you can actually say the "I dos," preventing all kinds of bad, hasty, alcohol-fueled decisions, but potentially fouling up a wedding for a couple who weren't so good on the details.

There are only so many times the church pianist can play "I Love You Truly" and "We've Only Just Begun." I'd be willing to bet the farm she didn't have three days' worth of love songs in her repertoire.

Fortunately, Mississippi lawmakers, in their wisdom, provided this lovely couple with an out. A circuit judge could waive the waiting period. Providing, of course, there's a good reason. A church full of people and ice melting in the punchbowl is a pretty good reason.

The judge, though, couldn't just waive marital waiting periods willy-nilly. Testimony had to be heard. So the court reporter got out a fresh tape and looked like she was on her marks and ready to run, so to speak.

And the judge began calling witnesses.

The preacher.

The bride-to-be.

They were both good and sober, which is something judges look for in witnesses, especially ones who are about to be married.

And then the bridegroom stepped up to the witness stand. The circuit judge questioned him on his sobriety and why they didn't remember that people have to have licenses to be legally married. Which, by the way, are pretty easy to get. It's harder to get a learner's permit to drive a car than it is to get a license to make a decision that is supposed to last the rest of your days.

So why, the judge asked, should he grant this request and waive the waiting period that was required back then so this couple could enter into happily wedded marital bliss?

"Because," the bridegroom said, "I love her and I can't wait no more, your honor."

The courtroom was filled with smiles, and I could tell the circuit judge was stifling a giggle like a middle-schooler in health class.

And we all had to admit this was much better than the usual round of guilty pleas and requests for continuances and changes of venue.

The couple was granted their request. They didn't have to wait no more. They high-tailed it to the church, and I spent the afternoon imagining them having a wedding more memorable than it already was. I was hoping no one left the church, everyone enjoyed the reception, the cake wasn't dry and that no one blinked in the wedding pictures.

That wedding day was a couple of decades ago, give or take. I don't remember the names of the bride or her hubby and don't know what became of them.

My wish for them is that they're still in love, maybe with a houseful of kids who are driving them crazy being teenagers by now. I hope those two, that crazy couple without a marriage license on their wedding day, have had more joy than sorrow and more happiness than they ever thought possible on that day in court.

While love, true love, is worth waiting for, there came a time when they just couldn't wait no more.

Wedding planning

Weddings I attended as a girl were fairly simple affairs. There was a bride wearing a gown that her mama might have whipped up on the Singer sewing machine, something that started just beneath her chin and covered her arms to the wrist.

There was a groom, dressed in that day's tuxedo style: light blue with a ruffled shirt.

And there were a collection of family members in the wedding party. They would stand in a sober row in the wedding pictures.

The receptions had a cake, a bowl of fruit punch and maybe some mixed nuts.

Most of these weddings were Baptist rites of passage, so there wasn't any music at the reception. It might have led to dancing, and for Baptists of the 1970s, that was a chance not worth taking.

Let's just say that in forty years, the wedding pendulum has swung in the other direction.

One of my children, while I was working on a wedding issue of a magazine for my features editing day job, asked me how much a wedding costs.

Well, it depends.

Asking how much a wedding costs is like asking how much a car costs.

I once bought a hooptie car for $1,200. And I am sure there are even cheaper options out there. There are also Bentleys that cost upwards of $200,000.

They will both get you where you want to go. In the case of the hooptie, hopefully you didn't want to go too far.

Getting married can be done for the price of a license and your blood test, plus paying the preacher or the justice of the peace.

Or it can be done Kim Kardashian-style, with an engagement ring worth ten times the price of my house.

Both will get you equally married, and neither will ensure your union will be an enduring one.

Most weddings are somewhere between the extremes, enough hoopla to make a party and enough austerity to make sure someone wasn't in the poor house once the bills came in.

A receiving line, cake and punch they're not, though.

There is a couple in San Francisco who made a movie trailer to announce their "Boss Wedding." I would say I thought I was watching a Kanye West video. Because I did, plus why not mention Kanye since I already wrote about Kim?

There was a helicopter, limousine, aerial view of the city, a party scene and dance number. And they weren't even married yet.

Wedding planning, at least in my small town, was relegated to the florists and church hostesses. Now, it is a bit of an industry. Wedding planners sometimes are flown into town for events, and they are truly events.

They're not just celebrations of matrimony. They are celebrations of both halves of that couple. Personalities show through. Brides can have their favorite fast food on the reception buffet and no one bats an eye.

Grooms' cakes are turning into works of art, like something off a Food Channel TV show. There are Harry Potter cakes and U.S. Marine Corps cakes, appropriately emblazoned with "Semper Fi," and my favorite, a cake described in a wedding announcement back when every last detail was recorded in the newspaper for posterity.

This groom was a pharmacist, and the bride's mother had written, in her own hand, at length about the groom's cake, which was decorated with sugar pills. I laughed to myself and anyone else who would listen about the "prescription drugs" on the cake and wondered aloud whether they tossed a handful of valiums on top.

There are brides and grooms who bungee jump at their wedding. They ski. They parasail. They ride horses. If they were any more active, they would look like they were starring in feminine products commercials.

No more going to the bride's church as a knee-jerk reaction to where the wedding is. Destination weddings are in Disney World, on beaches, in Las Vegas. And this isn't eloping. The entire wedding party goes.

The wedding gowns are also high-ticket items, especially if you consider they might only be worn one time. I have my gown packed in a box under my stairs, waiting to be called into service by a child of mine or future daughter-in-law. It's supposed to be shrink-wrapped to keep it from yellowing, but I live hours from the dry cleaners who did the job. Besides, I don't even remember the name of the dry-cleaning business. If the gown yellows, it yellows.

Watch "Say Yes to the Dress" sometime. I have driven cars worth way less than the cost of these dresses. Families take up collections for these gowns, some of which, by the way, would have been scandalous in my hometown back in the day. Watch the show and you'll think some want to be hoochie mamas in white.

Some of the gowns are breathtaking, though. Gorgeous. Glamorous. And then you see the price. That's the breathtaking part.

Then there are the receptions. Honestly, I have seen the photographic evidence of quite a few high society weddings, and my first thought after seeing the photos of the food at these wing-dings is that I don't know enough people who are getting married.

I'm thinking that wedding crashing could be an inexpensive date night.

As for the brides and grooms, be happy, and let your wedding help in your happiness. If your wedding planning is stressing you out, imagine how stressed you'll be when the bills arrive.

Happily ever after

I love a good happily ever after story.

I'm a sucker for them, ever since I was a little girl. Every good princess story involved a happily ever after moment when the prince and his princess ride off, post-wedding ceremony, into the sunset.

Life is good. No fussing. No fighting. No days when the princess is so tired from raising young royals that she only remembers to shave one of her legs. No belches or wind-passing from the princely hubster.

Of course, you realize this only happens in fairytales.

In real life, your prince won't only get sick; he'll projectile vomit.

You will be bored sometimes and aggravated sometimes. So will he.

You will question what heck was going through your head when you said your vows. So will he.

The plumbing will flood your castle.

The kingdom will have a financial crisis or two.

The carriage might get repossessed.

Marriage, as it turns out, sometimes is not all it's cracked up to be. It doesn't always live up to the happily ever after storylines.

Sometimes it's unhappily ever after, at least 50 percent of the time, according to divorce statistics. And sometimes that unhappily ever after comes at you fast.

Recently, *USA Today* reported that a Delta flight from Atlanta to Costa Rica was diverted to the Cayman Islands because a couple on their honeymoon got into a drunken fight.

At least they got diverted somewhere nice. My first thought upon reading this breaking news story was that I'd have rather gone to the Caymans anyway, but that's just me. My second thought was that there are better ways of getting there.

Somehow you have an inkling that this couple, with the ink still damp on their marriage license, who couldn't hold it together past day one of the honeymoon, might be in for a little more relationship drama before all's said and done.

Unless you are part of one of those celebrity couples that goes by one name like Brangelina, it's probably a relationship red flag if USA Today is writing word number one about your honeymoon. You know the headline is not going to say, "Couple on honeymoon so in love and having best time."

But sometimes marriages do meet the happily ever after standard. Just not how you'd imagine.

It's not about the ring

Men and women are different. I know this may come as shocking news, but they are.

Here is exhibit A in a display of supporting evidence. Recently, I've heard multiple conversations about a Dear Abby letter.

In this letter, a wife wrote that she has hinted to her husband that she wants an engagement ring. They have been married for 40 years, but she never got a diamond even though they have the money for it.

She has hinted, shown him jewelry catalogs, asked her sister-in-law to tell him she wants a rock and all but driven him to the jewelry store, but nothing.

He's oblivious, she wrote, and she's ready to pull the plug on 40 years of marriage over this.

The men I know who commented on this said, "She has the money. She should just go out and buy her own diamond ring."

They also said they couldn't believe a woman who has been married 40 years would end a marriage over something as trivial as a ring. But I, and probably all the women I know, would say it's not about the diamond and was never about the diamond. It's about her feelings. And about her husband acting like an old goat.

Sometimes, when women want something, it is not really about whatever we say we want. It's about those we love thinking of us and showing their love by doing whatever it is we want. If we have to ask, fine, but us not asking and our loved ones figuring things out on their own, is, like the credit card commercial says, priceless.

If one of my sons mows the yard without being asked, well, I am just feeling the love. The shorter grass says, "I love you, mom. Thank you for being my mother. I hail your mothering by trimming the ends of the grass so the neighbors don't think our house is unkempt."

But back to the letter. Abby said this woman should just go buy herself a diamond ring and not let it negatively affect her marriage.

I have news for this couple. Call me a used-to-be-married marriage counselor.

This woman has given her husband 40 years. And he knows she wants a ring.

What's negatively affecting the marriage is a husband who's eaten 40 years of dinners and worn 40 years of clean clothes who somehow cannot get himself to get this woman a ring, not even from the Home Shopping Network, for crying out loud.

The value of that ring's not the ring. It's just a token made out of rock and metal. The value of it is in the love of the giver.

Buying your own engagement ring is sad. The letter writer really just wanted a little bit of a fuss made over her. She wanted to think that, to her husband of 40 years, she was worth some effort.

"But," said a male friend, "the man's not a mind reader."

"What she needs to do is get in his face," he said. "She needs to say, 'You know what would make me happy? You getting me a diamond ring. It is always something I have wanted, and it means enough to me that I am leaving you if I don't get one."

"Yeah, but," I said, "threatening someone with the ultimatum of buying a ring or getting a divorce just takes the romance out if it."

"You always have 'yeah, buts," he replied. "But you don't know his side of it because he's the one who has to pick up the newspaper and see a letter about his not buying her a ring in the newspaper."

Which, by the way, is what my mama would have called a "fine how-do-you-do."

Finding out that your significant other has problems with you by reading about it in the newspaper is a bad way to start out your day.

My male friend continued, "You don't know what else he is doing. He could be taking her on vacations or fixing up their house and he's thinking those are ways of showing her how much love he has for her, only those don't mean anything to her."

What says, 'I love you,' to her is the ring.

For others it could be time spent together or affection or sweet talk.

Everyone has his or her own way of hearing "I love you," and each of us has a unique way of saying it. Sometimes it just gets lost in translation, though.

Also, this is a heck of a curve ball she is throwing. I suspect it took forty years to get to this point of "Get me a ring or I am leaving you."

She married who she married. He's not a romantic, thoughtful guy, probably never was, probably hasn't been for a few decades and most likely will not change. And she has hit the point of having a belly full of it.

That's why, in relationships, we have to decide what we can live with, not just for today, but for 40 years. Decide what you can forgive, because if you are in a long-term relationship, rest assured there will have to be some forgiving going on. By both parties.

It's give and take. Push and pull. Compromise and meeting half way, or maybe more than half way.

Relationshipwise, whether it's with a significant other, your parents or your child, let's agree to do a couple of things to meet half way.

Ask for what you want, but also anticipate what would bring a smile to that person's face, and do that.

It takes a little effort, but it's probably cheaper than counseling.

Part II

Money and Other Reasons To Holler

Don't settle

There are these games people play on Facebook.

Give yourself advice in two words is one of them. If your future self could jump into a Delorean and travel back in time to tell your past self two life-changing words, what would you say?

If I could do that, I would tell myself these two words: "Don't settle."

Don't settle.

Imagine how not settling would change your life.

How many times have you sold yourself short by settling for less because you thought settling was the best you could do?

Did you take career paths because they were doable, and so what if they didn't exactly set your world on fire?

Did you date or even marry men who were not terrific, not that nice to you, not all that and a bag of chips, just because something inside said, "Yep, he's about the best I can get." And you know he's not the best out there, but he puts up with you, so you adjust, figure this is as good as it's going to get for you and go on with something that's OK at best.

Did you talk yourself out of pursuing a dream?

Not go on some trip of a lifetime?

Pass up training or the pursuit of a degree just because you thought you weren't smart enough, that your education wasn't worth the cost or that you're too old?

Congratulations. You've settled.

Settling is our way of telling ourselves we're less than everyone else.

We tell ourselves that happiness is for other people.

Great careers that leave us energized and hopeful and excited are for everyone else; we get the dead-end drudgery jobs.

We'll never be rich, we tell ourselves. Not only will wealth never happen, paying off the credit cards or the Camry will never happen.

And the guy who you aren't crazy about, the one who treats you badly but the one you put up with because he's the best you think you can get, and otherwise you'd be alone.

It's all settling.

It's not what you want, but instead of embracing change, which can scare the pants off you, you make do. Any time you live in a place you hate, work at a job you dread, date a man who doesn't treat you in the manner that, deep down, you know you deserve but think you won't ever find anyone better, or decide you will never earn more, do more or be more than you are right now, you are settling.

Which is, well, a little unsettling.

We all do it, and it's something that needs to stop.

Every part of our lives should feed our souls. Our jobs, our relationships, our surroundings and our thoughts and dreams should all leave us with more energy, not less. They should fill us, not drain us.

So how do we stop settling?

First, we have to see ourselves as worthy.

For me, it was asking myself whether what I was doing, thinking or putting up with was something I would want for my daughter.

Would I want her thinking she didn't deserve more? Or putting up with a bad relationship? Or doing a job just because she didn't think she was capable of anything better?

Then it means giving up feeling like a victim. Because victims settle all the time. They have excellent reasons to settle, and they'll be happy to list them for you.

I know because I have been the queen victim of my own pity party. I would come up with all sorts of reasons why I could have a great life if only. If only I had more money. If only I weighed less or looked prettier. If only there was more time in the day. If only life wasn't so hard.

If only. Ban those words from your vocabulary.

Make your dreams happen in spite of whatever you think holds you back. No if onlys.

Because life is hard, and circumstances are never perfect or pretty or easy. You have to dream and go and do anyway.

Take what you have and improve it.

Things you can't improve you might need to part with. Maybe you need to change jobs or go back to school or set up some boundaries that toxic people who drain you of your energy can't cross.

Life won't magically get perfect. Instead, life gets a little better each day. Baby step by baby step.

Not settling is not easy, but so what?

If not settling was easy, no one would settle. Think how that might shake up the world.

Digging out

I never started out thinking I would find myself in a hole, but there I was.

In a hole, and all of it from my own digging.

Out of balance is what I was, and what my checkbook was.

There was work, all I could stand and some I couldn't, plus a part-time job, but there was always more month than money.

The bills were never-ending. So were the needs and the wants.

The harder I worked, the farther behind I fell. Tired, out of shape and overweight because I was eating all the wrong things at the wrong times for the wrong reasons and not moving unless walking from my desk to the vending machine counts. And, by the way, it doesn't.

I was working more hours, but it was like running in place. I was wearing myself out and getting nowhere.

Life was out of whack.

And I desperately wanted things to be in whack.

I wanted to feel like I was good enough to measure up to the ridiculously high standards I was holding myself to, standards that were reserved only for me. I'd never be that demanding of anyone else.

I wanted to feel worthy and have life under control. I wanted to feel good about where life and our finances were going. All that, and I wanted to sleep. Badly.

And those wants and wishes, as it turns out, were the first shovelfuls on my way to digging out of a self-dug hole.

The first step to getting out of a hole is to stop digging. Whatever you are doing to put yourself at a lower level, just stop it.

This is not as simple as it sounds, because it requires change. Maybe change on your part, and maybe change on the parts of those near and dear.

Changing habits will be involved, and anyone who's ever gone on a diet can tell you how quick and easy that is. You might have to learn to tell others no, and you might have to learn to say that to yourself, too. And mean it.

The next step is even more difficult and painful. It is finding out just how deep the hole you've dug is.

I am not going to pretend that I haven't shut my eyes and winced when looking at my checking account balance online. By the way, shutting your eyes tightly will not add money to your account.

And chanting, "Please work, please work, please work," when you've just swiped your debit card at the gas pump will not make it work. I know because I've tried.

You are going to have to face facts. Write down exactly what you owe. You might be surprised – things may not be as dire as you think. I've checked on the life span of a car loan to learn I was less than six payments away from holding the title myself.

Once you know where you are and have hit the brakes on your descent, you need a plan. A way out. A way up.

Look at the debts you owe. Find out which ones are the smallest and pay them off first, even if they are not the highest interest ones. Why? Because paying off a small account will give you some emotional momentum, It starts you on your way.

Then you take the funds that were going to that account and put them toward the others you were paying the bare minimum on.

I was taking action. But action alone wasn't enough for me, because my attitudes about money were as troubled as my financial statement. I was operating from a mindset of not enough, of surviving and not thriving.

Years of scrimping had saved me some money, but they had not removed the worries over money.

What had to change was my mindset. Changing it meant thinking about what I have and feeling a strong sense of gratitude for all that I had. My car may have been older but it was reliable, so I gave thanks for it. My home may need repairs, but it is where our family grew up and is warm in the winter, cool in the summer.

No matter your situation, there is something you can be thankful for, even if it is gratitude for the situation not being worse. Because things can always get worse. Even if you think you are at rock bottom, you can be thankful that the only direction you can go is up.

Imagine how you would feel if your money problems were gone. You had enough money to buy whatever you needed and extra for things you wanted. You had no feelings of want or lack.

Yeah, I know this is going to require some imagination, but do it. Imagine the lightness of not hauling around all your worries.

Then realize that you can have that mindset now, and not just when you finish digging out.

Worry does not put money in your pocket. Worse, it might take money out of it in terms of stress and the toll it takes.

Act like you are thriving. Don't look at things and think you cannot afford them. Instead, think that this is not how you choose to spend your money.

Chances are, you didn't get in a hole with one big bad decision. You got where you are with lots of little bad decisions. You will get out of the hole with lots of good choices. You didn't get where you are overnight, but over time you can be where you want to be, and with good personal choices, deserve to be.

Patterns

Nobody ever sets out to be broke. No one wants to be stressed over money.

Yet it happens anyway. To pretty much all of us.

I promise you, worrying over whether there would be the right amount of month to fit the money was not what I set out to do. But if everyone wound up doing what they wanted to do when they were children, this would be a world full of ballerinas and presidents of the United States, all of whom are independently wealthy.

The other thing is, worry over money is relative, and that doesn't mean your cousin hits you up for a loan at the family Christmas gathering. What that means is that whether you have two nickels to rub together or a Scrooge McDuck swimming pool of money, it can still be worried over. It can still rob your sleep and give you wrinkles. It is a vicious cycle, the part about the wrinkles, because Botox is not cheap.

There have been months I have wondered how we would eat and live indoors and yet not lost an inordinate amount of sleep. After all, sleep's free so you might as well enjoy it when you're broke.

Then there are people who have not only a roof over their heads but steak in the refrigerator and a Jaguar in the garage, yet they ulcerate themselves with worry over their net worth and cash flow.

Money, despite quotes to the contrary, is not evil. It's not even gold anymore. Just paper.

It's only a tool we use to get things. Instead of tilling the ground or clubbing a critter ourselves, we use money to pay for and fuel our cars to drive over to Mac's Fresh Market to get veggies we didn't pick and critters we didn't club, also using money.

Money isn't good, either, although it can be used to do good in the world. I see money as neutral. It doesn't have a conscience any more than the Phillips head screwdriver in the kitchen junk drawer knows right from wrong. They are both tools and can either be used well or, well, not.

I once read that if a problem can be solved with money, then it isn't really a problem. That can be true in some cases. But money can solve a money problem, right?

Maybe in the short term. Not necessarily in the long.

I've also heard the criticism that putting more money toward public education, for example, is just throwing money at a problem. And then I have thought how awesome it would be if the world would just throw money at one of my problems. Or one of yours.

Throwing money at it might not fix the problem, but it sure would be entertaining.

Here's the thing, though. Even if we end up with the world throwing money at our problems, each of us follows a pattern when it comes to money. And changing it is a bit of a challenge, because it is engrained. We don't even realize we have patterns, sometimes. We get these mindsets from our childhoods, and our parents' and grandparents' childhoods. It's how we view money and how we use it.

Our patterns are our comfort zone with money, and even though it might not be comfortable, even though it might cause everything from crow's feet to a sleepless night, they are what we know and what we're used to.

Ever wonder why it is that some Power Ball winners take home millions after taxes yet wind up as poor or poorer than before?

It's not that they squandered their money, gave it to every relative with a hand out or just made horribly stupid investments. They probably did all those things, but those decisions were just symptoms of the pattern we each have.

Way too many times, I have been getting by with exactly enough and not a penny more, leaving me to wonder if somehow I like the feeling of the day being saved in the nick of time.

There are those of us who feel loved, albeit for a brief amount of time, when we get stuff. More stuff equals more love. Also more bills.

Maybe there are feelings of guilt associated with money, or fear. Or maybe a smoothie made out of all these and more. We're each our own blend of crazy when it comes to money.

Here are my thoughts on this as a woman who's coming to grips with Oeth-onomics.

1. **You are where you are because you allowed it to happen.** Don't blame someone else, because even if they did screw up your finances, you let it happen. This is a hard one, but take responsibility for where you are now.

2. **But don't beat yourself up for it.** There is a line between owning up to your responsibility for where you are and berating yourself for that. I had some excellent reasons for bad financial choices, including some that were made out of love. You got yourself here, but the up side is that you will also be the one to get yourself someplace better. The world is a rough enough place without you adding to the wallops, so don't.

3. **Respect yourself by respecting your money.** When you respect your money, you have a better life, in turn giving yourself a little R-E-S-P-E-C-T. go to the library and check out some books on finances, investing, budgeting or whatever makes your eyes light up. When you respect yourself and your money, you tend to save. You tend to pay your bills on time. You tend

to make smarter choices. But you can't respect the money if you first don't respect yourself.

4. **Be accountable.** Find someone you can trust and tell them your goals. Just telling someone else your hopes and dreams is magical. They become real when they're spoken, no matter how hard it can be sometimes to speak them into being. It's your dreams' first step out of your imagination.

5. **Stop worrying.** Pray over your problems if you are the praying kind, and then let them go. Worrying is only going to give you an ulcer. Put that energy into being proactive instead, because that can and usually does make a positive difference. Stewing over your troubles never does.

6. **Save.** Even if it is the change between the couch cushions or a few bucks out of every paycheck. See if your employer offers a 401(k) plan and sign up. Not only will saving result in a little nest egg for you, but it does something positive to your outlook.

7. **Give it away.** Here's something even more positive for the way you see the world. Help others. Even if you can't give much, even if you are sure it won't make a difference, do it anyway. It will make a difference with at least one person, and that person is you. There is always someone less fortunate than yourself, so get your focus off your own troubles. This is good for the soul.

8. **Be grateful for what you have.** Until you are grateful for the resources you already have, you will never pull yourself out of whatever tailspin you are in. There's an old hymn about counting your blessings, naming them one by one, so do that. Make a list of your resources, your blessings, your assets – whatever you'd like to call them – and be thankful for them. Before your feet even hit the floor in the morning, give thanks for the blessings in your life. It will cut your problems down to size like nothing else.

9. **Be grateful for life's problems.** Yeah, right, you say. But nothing schools you like a problem. I worry about people who have never faced down a problem, because they haven't learned very much in life. It is much easier to give thanks for problems and heartaches and bad choices when they are in the rearview mirror, but once they are, you should be the wiser for them.

10. **Live rich.** There are wealthy people who can't do this, and poor ones who can. Go figure. Living rich does not mean driving a Porsche and living in a mansion. It means not worrying over money. It means appreciating what you have and the people you love and all the things that money can't buy. It means being happy with what you have instead of maxing out your charge cards. I don't know that I will ever be rich, but I try to live rich.

Credit cards
(may they burn in hell)

The offers came pouring in. Fantastic plastic. No annual fee. Low, low rates. Thousands of dollars in credit available.

And these were all addressed to an 18-year-old with no job.

This may be one of those times when I overstepped my boundaries as a mama of some children who are old enough to vote, but my Dear Sons never got those offers. I got the mail and shredded them before they had a chance to sign up.

Because credit can get you into a world of trouble. At a young age, I might add.

The system is really perverse. To have good credit, you have to have credit.

If you pay off a credit card and close the account, you hurt your credit score. If you don't use credit and pay as you go, you hurt your credit score. It's like the whole object of the game is to get you using the cards and paying the credit card companies money every month.

Oh, wait. That is the object of the game.

I've had my own battles with them. I was way behind in the game when we had to charge groceries to get by, and medical bills, but I paid them off and got the accounts back out of the red-hot-screaming-emergency zone. I am just happy there aren't debtors' prisons anymore.

Here are two pieces of information for those of you who appreciate irony.

- ✓ You need to have a credit card to function. Renting a car and getting a hotel room are pretty much impossible unless you have one.
- ✓ But you have to use it sparingly.

It's like saying, "Here, have some dark chocolate, or crack, or whatever other addictive thing you can think of," and ladies, you all know you each have your own little addictions. It may not be crack cocaine, and let's hope it's not, but it's somewhere between that and M&Ms or your morning coffee.

So just picture having that thing that you crave. It is glorious.

But you can't use all of it. You can only use a little. Maybe.

Careful, don't go overboard. If you use too much of whatever your magic addictive stuff is, you can't get any more of the magic addictive stuff. And, by implication, it makes you a bad person, or at least makes you feel that way.

Ironic, no? But that is how credit cards work. It's actually past irony and in one of those rings of hell Dante wrote about.

Yes, I said it, credit cards were invented by Satan.

It's a proven fact, though, that it is easier to overspend with a credit card. You know you are not getting a bill before the next month, but Christmas is right now, and you never know. You might get hit by a bus. The Mayans might have been right, but just off on the dates. Go for the gusto while you still can.

According to research by *Time* and *Money* magazines, the average credit card debt for Americans is nearly $10,000, and much of that is for unnecessary purchases. However, what about when you need groceries or a root canal or the lights on. Well, that may not be as reckless in your mind as hitting the boutiques to charge some retail therapy, but charging necessities can whip up on your credit score.

As can paying off an account and then closing it.

As odd as it may sound, keeping a small amount or a zero balance on your cards and keeping them open gives you a better credit score than just closing the account after you have paid the card off. I found this out after closing two accounts on the advice of a bank manager in order to raise my score. Instead, it plummeted. Which goes to show you that even financial professionals aren't quite sure of the alchemy involved in creating a credit score.

More proof that credit cards were invented by Satan.

However, there are ways to not let Lucifer win this game. Here are a few tips:

- ✓ **Pay off your balances in full and on time.** If you can't pay off the balance in full, pay as much as you can over the minimum.
- ✓ **Do not pay only the minimum.** Since they don't have debtors' prisons and workhouses anymore, paying the minimum is as close as the system can get. You'll pay far more than you charged and over a much longer period of time.
- ✓ **Don't max out your cards.** I have been there and done that, so I can tell you that is not a good idea. Credit score-wise, it is better to have two credit cards with balances than one that is at its limit, even if the amount owed is the same because scoring agencies look at the debt-to-available credit ratio. If you have used all your available credit, then Satan's a happy camper and your score is getting poked by a pitchfork.
- ✓ **Don't hit the 50 percent limit on your cards.** When you are more than half way to your limit, your score will go down.
- ✓ **Get a check-up with the devil once a year.** Each of the three credit score agencies of the apocalypse will give you a free credit report each year. How nice of them.
- ✓ **Do a little visualization.** When you pay those bills on time each month, before you drop the bills in the mailbox old-school style or click

"confirm" on the cards' websites, imagine how great it will feel to have them under control and then paid off. Try to have and enjoy that feeling now rather than later. Worrying won't lower your balances, but being proactive will.

Bills, bills, bills

An empty mailbox is a happy mailbox.

That had been my motto for a while. Because my mailbox was seldom empty. Bill was in it, along with several of his friends, ready to throw a surprise party for me when I got the mail.

Surprise!

Bills were something that tended to multiply for us. Robbing Peter to pay Paul was one thing, but we were telling Paul the check was in the mail. Hoping things get better while taking the same actions didn't change the fact that Bill and his friends kept showing up every month.

Ignoring Bill and his buddies also didn't work. They just grew while we tried to pretend they didn't exist.

What also didn't work was that my other half didn't want to talk about money. Ever. It's hard to be on the same page when the books are shut tight.

Bill didn't only show up in the mailbox, though. He called sometimes. And we'd dodge his calls because we didn't want to hear what he had to say.

We both knew the truth that we were hanging on by an unraveling thread financially. And with one of us in denial and the other trying to skinflint us out of debt, we went as a couple from not being on the same page to not even being in the same library.

Does any of this sound familiar? I know that we weren't the only family Bill would throw surprise parties for. If he's been showing up at your place and you'd like to make his visits less frequent, here are a few tips from someone who's working to make her finances less of a worry and more a source of peace.

Figure out where you are. This was painful for me. I didn't want to see my bank balance some days, and I still don't at times. Look anyway. Write down what you owe, when loans will be paid in full and what assets you have. This may not be as awful as you think. I did this within the past year and realized that our finances were improving within a two-year period, when two loans would be paid off.

Don't come in with a bad attitude. I have never liked numbers or math. I scored a 4.0 in strategic financial analysis in college, but I have never liked dealing with my own finances. Those are personal. Anyhow, for years I would face this thinking that I was ill-equipped to deal with the numbers. That's defeatist thinking, so don't try that escape route. If you can add and subtract, you can work out a plan to give Bill and his buddies the heave-ho.

Don't hide from Bill. Take his calls, too. This comes from my oldest son, who is a loan company manager. He is a helpful person by nature, and he is more than willing to work with someone who calls him, wanting to get his payments caught up. Someone he has to hunt down, though, isn't as likely to gain his help. Answering calls from bill collectors and sending in payments, even the minimums, show your intention is to honor your word and make payments as agreed.

Get on the same page. Getting out of debt is vastly easier if the whole family is involved, including any youngsters around. Without teamwork, you're going to feel like you are up against everyone else in the house, and that is only because you are.

Rein in spending. Let's all holler, "Whoa, Nelly!" To get out of debt, you first have to stop adding to the number of Bill's friends. Stop using your credit cards (one neat way to do this, if impulse buying is a problem, is to put them in a plastic container, fill the container with water and pop it in the freezer. You'll have to wait until the cards thaw to use them). And do not darken the door of a payday loan business unless you literally do not know where your next meal is coming from.

Make being a tightwad a game. Thinking of ways to save can actually be fun when everyone is involved. At our house, we've done this in all kinds of ways, from stretching leftovers to trying to get the last drops out of a bottle of shampoo to using book-leasing websites such as Chegg.com for my college students.

Save. Yes, this sounds crazy when you are trying to get out of debt, but this will help you psychologically. And financially. You will have cash that can be used in an emergency instead of whipping out a credit card (may they burn in hell).

Get professional help. You may feel like I mean the psychiatric kind, but find a financial counselor you can trust and get an outsider's opinion. A different outlook will help you feel like you are not about to go off the fiscal cliff.

Eat a Whammy. There's an old saying about eating an elephant, but I don't much care for that on my dinner plate. Over at Burgers & Blues, they have a three-pound hamburger called the Whammy. It's one of those meals you eat on a dare. Finish it and a pound of fries and all the other trimmings within 30 minutes and it is free. How do people finish that enormous meal, one that has more meat in it for one meal than my family would eat in three? They eat it one bite at a time. Granted, they're big bites. Just know that you didn't get into this mess into one day. It'll take constant, consistent bites to get you past the Whammy your finances are in.

Set some benchmarks. You could start from where you are now, in a pile of debt, and go to where you want to be, but that seems like a long journey. Set some smaller goals along the way and celebrate when you reach them. Just don't celebrate by going into more debt.

Dig faster. Find alternate sources of income and pour that extra moolah into the debt. Not everyone can do this, either due to family responsibilities or just plain exhaustion, but it is a thought. If you have a hobby or a skill, you might turn that into extra cash, and who knows, maybe your own business.

Be grateful. Chances are you have more resources than you realize. You will feel defeated if you only think about the bills and the burdens. Start your day, and I mean before your feet hit the floor, by being grateful for all the blessings in your life.

I am still on this journey, but I can tell you that my finances are better than when I started. Life would have been easier had I won the lottery, but I would have learned nothing and most likely would have made bad decisions with my millions.

Broke but not broken

I've been broke a time or twelve.

And at most of those times, I had a full-time job in management, a 401(k), a house, children, a husband, parents and bills.

Lord, did I have bills.

There were a couple of times when I was broke that I felt broken, though, and that is Mach 5 in the world of no money, honey.

Broke is when you don't have money, and that is, what they call in financial circles, a liquidity crisis.

If I had to come up with cash, I could have, but who wants to dip into retirement savings for a trip to the grocery store or a few gallons of gas. Do that enough times and you'll be saying, "Thank you for shopping at Wal-Mart" during your golden years.

I also had equity in my house, but that's a long term investment that's hard to convert into a tank of gas or a loaf of bread.

Broken is when you feel that not only does your cash flow have no liquid to it but that it is a reflection on you, your choices and your abilities or a lack thereof.

There was the time I was tired after a long day at work and was on my way to visit my mother, who was in a nursing home at the time, and then give my father a ride home, get my sweet babies to bed and start the whole process over again the next day.

To say, at that time, I was holding things together would have been true, I suppose, but I was holding them together with bubble gum, Scotch tape and spit, along with some prayers.

So I decided I really needed a Coca-Cola, which has been known to fix whatever's ailed me. I'm a journalist by trade, and journalists do have a reputation for downing plenty of caffeine to get through the day, night, afternoon or the next hour.

We drink coffee like it's water, which, technically, it is, only run through those ground beans of life and energy.

That night, though, I wanted a Coca-Cola, with all the caffeine and all the sugar, The Wal-Mart over in Pearl at that time had a Coke machine that would trade you a soda for 35 cents. I knew that because I had a lot that ailed me then, so knowing where cheap Coca-Cola was had immediate benefits.

I needed some energy on that evening, and there I was in the Wal-Mart parking lot after dark, searching every hidey-hole in my handbag for 35 cents not counting pennies.

I found a quarter.

Broken to me was in the moments that followed, sticking my arm between the car seats front and back and digging around under seats and pulling up floor mats in search of 10 more cents.

I wanted to cry but I didn't have the energy. I was the employed member of the family and the holder of a college degree, and I knew life should have been a whole heck of a lot better than praying someone dropped a coin in the past so I could drink a Coke in the present.

I could pretend to the rest of the world that all was well, to the point that I was quite good at it. I put forth some Academy Award performances. But there's no lying to yourself about it. When you are overjoyed to find a sticky nickel under a car seat, you're broken.

And also broke.

I found enough change for a Coca-Cola that night, which, at the time, was proof to me that there is a God. Jesus handing me a Coca-Cola wouldn't have impressed me more.

Things didn't improve, at least not right away.

I wish I could say that, like magic, my checking account was overflowing after realizing my broken state, but that's not how that works.

No, I have had plenty of other moments where I realized a need, either financial or emotional. Or both.

Just like that night in my 10-year-old Saturn, when I was digging for dirty pocket change, needs will hit you with a one-two punch. Broke and broken.

In my case, I drank the Coca-Cola like it was Dom Perignon. And I went about doing the best I could for my parents and for my husband and children. The best I could, I realized, wasn't perfect, nor did it have to be. It was the best at that moment.

Best, though, got better. Slowly.

There were no winning lottery tickets in my purse, and the Prize Patrol didn't have my address on their GPS. Plenty of times I have hit points where I wondered how in the world the house note would be paid or the kids would go to college. But there are three degrees between the older two sons, plus a master's for their mama, and I'm sitting inside that same house.

Your best, as it turns out, can be enough, if you keep giving it every day.

There are still lean weeks when we're coasting to pay day and ready for that eagle to fly on Wednesday instead of Friday, but I'm working on making those few and far between.

The difference is that now, even if broke happens, it doesn't have to mean I am broken in spirit, nor does it have to mean that for you. There's a saying that if money would fix your problems, then they aren't real problems. The first time I heard that, I thought, "Money would fix my money problems," but I was wrong.

Brokenness of spirit had to be fixed before the broke part. Otherwise, the broke part would show back up again, turning up like a bad penny.

Decide that you are worthy and capable and deserving of good things and good situations. A lack of money does not mean you are a bad person, or a stupid one, and a lack of money does not have to be permanent.

Broke does not mean you are broken. It just means some things in your life need to be fixed.

Get your broken spirit fixed first, and then set about fixing the rest.

The Pink Mafia

Do you have people?

I do. I have so many people, I might never need to walk into a department store, drug store, boutique or Wal-Mart again.

It's because I have quite a few female friends who sell things either on the side or as their main income. They sell Avon and Rodan & Fields and Mary Kay. They sell handbags and totes from Thirty-One and jewelry from Premiere and Noonday Collection. They sell shopping club memberships. They sell vitamins and Juice Plus and health food and diet aids and wraps that will take inches off. If the wraps and diet aids don't work, they have heavy-duty bad-mammer-jammer garments that hold everything in so nothing moves unless you want it to.

When I started Christmas shopping last year, I started shopping with them first, and most of them, I can either Facebook message or go to their websites to order stuff. The Boss Man at the office is never the wiser unless he reads this.

They are also so appreciative. I have yet to get a hug from going to a Wal-Mart, but you might even get a party and snacks and good conversation along with your hug around the neck with one of these ladies.

They also use the stuff they sell, so I figure they know what they are talking about.

So yes, I have people. And I have been people for others. I had two tours of duty as an Avon lady and a short time with Mary Kay, so I can talk about them.

Every year, thousands of men and women sign up to be consultants, distributors, representatives and what-have-you for different multi-level marketing companies, each hoping for wealth.

Here is the deal, based on my experience and those of friends. Not that I want to rain on your wealth parade, but drip, drip, drip.

The times that I sold Avon, once when I was a college student and again when I was a young mother, it was a good way to make a little extra cash. It helped finance some of our Christmases and helped make the money stretch. I had to watch myself, because I'd be tempted to spend my profits out of the company catalog, but that was really the only downside. I didn't have a lot of risk, but I didn't make crazy money, either.

I wasn't making quit-your-day-job money. Instead, I was making enough where I had a little extra at the end of the month.

I had to quit when family and work responsibilities left me exhausted enough that I knew something had to go. And Avon was it. I remember thinking at the time that I would have paid someone $20 just so I could take a nap on a Sunday afternoon. Too much moonlighting will do that to you.

Another time, I was working, finishing a graduate degree and thought maybe selling Mary Kay would be a good idea. If you haven't guessed, overestimating my time management skills is a teeny-weeny weakness of mine. I quickly realized that I didn't have the cash to invest in the Mary Kay products I would have to buy, plus I ran through most of my friends.

That's the thing about these companies. Friends get hard to come by when you start selling things or inviting them to listen to business opportunities. You might as well be yelling "Fire!" because they take off running just the same.

As a jogging buddy of mine once said, "If I have to go to one more jewelry or makeup party this month, I will be flat broke."

Then there is the selling part. I was never good at that. Being good at selling things is a gift, one that I never got. Some companies call it "sharing," and who doesn't like to share?

Call it "sharing," "caring" or "overbearing," it's selling.

That's the marketing part. The multilevel part is where the money comes in because you sign up more people to sell, only you make a commission on what they sell, so you really have to hope they have the gift.

There are those who do really well in these multilevel marketing businesses. I've met whole families who sell things, and there are a few who do really well. They have the company car, and one couple I know could pack up their kids and live anywhere they choose because their job is signing up people to sell, which they manage online. And that is great, but for every one of those, there are lots of others who just supplement the Christmas funds.

The times I signed up to sell stuff, I had good memories to push me forward. Back in the day, the Avon lady and the Mary Kay lady were about the most glammed-up women in town.

I have fond memories of going around to Tupperware parties my mother's friends would have. We kids would play in the back yard while the ladies got lessons in food freshness, and then there was always dessert afterward.

So who wouldn't want to sign up for that?

And then there is the idea of being able to balance your family with a job, back in the early 1970s, and now balance family and the day job. The selling jobs are pretty darned flexible.

This is why most of the people I know who sell stuff on the side are women. Men just don't multitask as well as women do. In general, men focus on one job at a time, not selling this and that and also working 40 hours a week somewhere else and keeping the house clean.

Women also buy into the dream. I've never gone to a convention, but they do have them, and judging from the pictures, they're like Disney World for grown people with a shot of Joel Osteen.

I've seen women who have come back from these, and they are pumped up. And you would be, too, if you got to wear a crown and evening gown while being motivated out the wazoo.

I don't know that I can truly imagine Moses coming off the mountaintop, but I suspect he was about as jazzed up as my friends who have come back from company conventions.

It's like joining the mafia, though. In the case of Mary Kay, a pink mafia. Not the killing and doing other illegal stuff parts, but the not ever leaving part. If love means never having to say you're sorry, then joining a multi-level marketing company means never having to say goodbye. You could say goodbye, but no one is going to think you mean it.

Nobody will kill you if you stop selling Mary Kay or Avon, for example, but you will hear from them from time to time. I haven't sold Avon in more than a decade, and I still get emails from them.

Just like Michael Corleone, just when you think you are out, they'll pull you back in. Or try to.

Having a side business can help if you are trying to pay down bills or save. And there are those who wind up with cars and make their side business into their main business.

They did that with lots of hard work, though.

Just know that these businesses, like pretty much anything else in life, aren't as easy as they sound. Anyone who's an achiever in a multi-level marketing business is there because she's worked hard and worked smart and is one heck of a manager.

Also, know what you will do with the profits.

If I have a regret from my Avon days, it is that I didn't save more of the additional cash I made. It just kept us closer to making ends meet. The sucking sound was our general household expenses taking in any additional money.

At the end of the day, it's all about whether a side selling business makes your life better, and only you can be the judge of that. If it makes you money and brings you happiness, and maybe a tiara or a pink car, then make it part of your financial plan.

Finding a sugar daddy

I was at the bank one day when I ran into a coworker. At the time, we knew there was a round of downsizings coming, and we all were thinking about the plan B we'd trot out if there was a Reduction In Force bullet with our names on it.

But my coworker, a man in his mid-50s who was a blend of pragmatism with a dash of curmudgeon thrown in, had an out-of-the-box idea.

"If it happens to you, what are you going to do?" he asked.

I had some ho-hum answer about finding another job as quickly as possible and living frugally. Typical boring old Annie Oeth stuff. Work hard. Play by the rules.

"No, if I were you," he said, shaking his head, "I'd find me a sugar daddy."

I didn't say anything right away because my brain was still trying to process what my ears had just heard.

Did he just say what I think he said? Did I just hear that?

"I mean it," he said. "Heck, if I wasn't married, I would find me a sweet little 90-year-old who's loaded."

You can't just unhear things like that.

I was alternately thinking of this man's wife being a candidate for sainthood and feeling sorry for any wealthy 90-year-old single women out there.

But, yes, apparently this is a career choice, or at least a dating choice, or maybe both, today. There are websites dedicated to this—seekingarrangement.com, sugardaddie.com, sugardaddyrelationship.com, and sugardaddytoday.com. I looked this up on the internet, and I feel so nasty now.

I looked at the area of Sugar Daddies seeking female "Sugar Babies" on one site, and all I can say is I feel even nastier. These men were a blend of middle-aged narcissists taking selfie pictures in their bathrooms and men who I am pretty sure posted the picture of the guy whose picture came with the snapshot holder in their wallets. Then there was an assortment of eightysomethings, including one who claimed to be a veteran of the Navy SEALs.

Not if I was starving. Not if I was living in a box. Not now, not ever could I imagine signing up for this insanity.

Never a "Sugar Baby," never, ever, ever. Living on a tight budget, all alone, save for your 15 cats, is a gigantic step up from that.

But sure enough, the idea seems to cross the minds of men who are middle-aged when they encounter single women. Because, while that bank lobby encounter was the first time I heard someone suggest finding a sugar daddy, it wasn't the last.

I think these men must at least entertain the idea of having a sugar daddy-style relationship, or else why would they joke about it?

Another time, I was at a sit-down meeting with my financial adviser, who was giving the Oeth-onomics system a once-over.

And he says, "OK, other than finding a sugar daddy, here are some things you can do to save for your children's college educations."

Since aging billionaires aren't just hanging around on every street corner, I started thinking about how I could tuck away a few dollars here and there.

Then one of my male besties tells me he spotted Mick Jagger around Jackson for the filming of the James Brown bio-pic "Get On Up."

"Now there's an older man with lots of money," he said. "You're just too lazy to find a sugar daddy."

And he was right, because I am pretty darned lazy.

Sugar daddies are not just a dime a dozen. To find a decent sugar daddy, I might have to shave my legs and pluck my eyebrows.

And the potential sugar daddies that are out there, I am thinking, are not on the lookout for women on the backside of 40 or the frontside of 50.

Heck, Joe Hundredaire down at the trailer park is thinking 20-somethings with less sense, fewer expectations and a whole lot less baggage.

Quite a few men in the middle years, if they are on the lookout for women to throw money at, think somewhere in the "young enough to be your daughter" range. Women in my age group need to be cruising the senior living apartments if we're looking for sugar daddies.

Even then, there is the old joke about, when a woman turns 40, exchanging her for two 20s. I didn't say it was a good joke, or a funny one, or that the man who said it didn't need to be swatted. Because he did.

Women would never make a joke about trading in one man for two others because that would be extra work. Why on earth would you want two men when one can be a handful? One extra man to leave socks and towels on the floor and whiskers in the sink. Two younger ones means you might as well be raising a couple of adult sons, and I mean barely adult.

The whole idea of the sugar daddy relationship makes me feel like taking a bath with a Brillo pad and Lava soap. If there is one thing that would feel worse than having someone pay to be with you, it would be feeling like you had to pay for company.

Here's a thought for you ladies who are seeking sugar daddies, and for those who, like me, just have to listen to jokes about finding one. How about, instead of using someone else for their money, we make our own?

I don't have much money, but I'm not going to desert myself if and when I get a few wrinkles. I mean, I haven't so far. I think my laugh lines are cute.

I only have to laugh at jokes I think are funny, and when bills are paid, as pleasant as that activity is, it is done by me.

I have become my own sugar daddy, although one who drives an economy car and mows her own lawn.

And for you sugar daddies out there, I know this whole shopping for women online must be like the creepy guy version of being a kid in a candy store, but paying for companionship, as if you could find company no other way, seems sad and empty. Sort of like the yang to the yin of having someone only interested in your company because of the reflection in your mirror.

Having a sugar daddy, or being one, isn't much of a plan. I think I'll stick to working hard, saving and knowing that my relationship is deeper than youth, looks or money.

Winning the lottery

The Louisiana Power Ball was at the hundreds of millions mark, and we in the newsroom were dreaming.

One of the crew was heading out to Mound, La., for a story about the craze of getting Power Ball tickets, and sure enough, when he got there, folks were lined up out the door and into the parking lot.

But our guy didn't just have a notebook and pen in his pocket. He had money from all of us. We had worked out a plan, and though the written agreement was not notarized, we felt like the arrangement would have kept us out of court if we had won and started squabbling over the money.

I guess you figured out we didn't win. You would have known if we had won because the newspaper wouldn't have come out that next day. Its staff of brand new millionaires would have been out celebrating instead of working.

I just had one share of our pool—one ticket—and I would have had about $4 million after taxes. $4 million.

That's beyond Monopoly money to me. Fathoming that kind of money boggles my little mind.

We shot a video of us all talking about what we would do with our money. I talked about paying off the kids' student loans, the house note and the car note, taking everyone to Disney World and having a beer.

It's the way my mind works. I don't think about buying a bigger, newer, better house and trading my Civic in for a sports car. That beer would have been just a regular old domestic light beer, too, although I might have splurged for a pricey craft beer.

But that wouldn't have put a dent in it.

Of course, it is easy for me to say that I would keep my simple tastes, and that I would keep working had I won the Power Ball. It is easy because I didn't win and because my odds of winning are probably along the lines of my chances of being struck by lightning.

Thank the Lord for that. On both counts.

Because I don't like the thought of being zapped from the heavens, and lottery winnings have been shown to wreck lives.

Statistics back this up. Someone wins the lottery, and pretty soon, there's a line of friends and relatives with their hands out. If they hear a "no," they get bent out of shape like the money was somehow due them by virtue of friendship or DNA. The lottery winners often start spending faster than the payments come in, and they forget that those winnings are taxed. They forget that enormous houses have enormous property taxes and upkeep costs. If they quit their jobs, they eventually miss them.

There are writers who say it is because those who win lotteries still have a mindset for a certain income, so the money goes because the winners are not thinking prosperous thoughts. And there may be some truth to that, but mostly lottery winners stand a chance to lose their money because they let that newfound money change who they are.

The money runs them, instead of the other way around. It defines where they live and what they do. They spend just because they can. And one day, maybe only subconsciously, they don't recognize who they are anymore.

Who knows? If I had won, maybe I would be drinking my Diet Coke from a golden goblet like the one Lil' Jon carries.

Lotteries can make you rich, but they won't keep you rich.

I've had a theory that the way to keep your lottery winnings, should you win, is to not tell anyone. OK, maybe your spouse, and this brings to mind an old joke.

A woman comes home and says to her husband, "Pack your bags! I've won the lottery!"

"That's great," he said. "Where are we going?"

"I don't know where *we're* going," she said, "but pack *your* bags, because you're going."

We can laugh about lottery winnings changing relationships, but they often do.

So a solid relationship with a spouse who won't call everyone in town to tell them the news is key, as is having a spouse who won't spend it in an afternoon. You also have to like who are and where you are and who you're with.

Then, lottery winner, you need to do some unglamorous things, like pay off your house note. Set up trusts to fund your children's educations. Give to your church or a charity. Save it so your golden years will truly be golden. But that's more easily said than done.

I did happen to win a lottery, and where are my winnings?

My oldest son gave me a Missouri lottery ticket as a gift tag on a Christmas present. And as I scratched away, I discovered I had a winner.

I spent $5 of my winnings on coins for my son's laundry and other $5 on coffee. My fortune squandered on clean clothes and caffeine.

Cheap retail therapy

OK, a spoiler alert. Retail therapy doesn't really make your problems go away.

I know from experience. I tried valiantly.

Retail therapy is akin to drinking to excess over your troubles. When you turn to the bottle, the next morning your troubles are still there, plus a hangover and the nagging question of what you said to whom.

Turning to food when life's hard doesn't work either, because the next day, you still have your problems plus a bigger butt.

This is something I think women try more often than men do.

We aren't happy with something, and to cope, we go shopping. I can remember in my younger days, buying a pair of shoes because I had an argument with a boyfriend. Buying shoes made me feel better for a brief while, but it didn't change that he was a Man Not Worth Having.

There are people who let retail therapy become an addiction. According to the website creditdonkey.com, some of the red flags of retail therapy becoming a problem include guilt after shopping (36.7 percent of their survey said they have this feeling) and hiding purchases from their families (20.5 percent of those surveyed do this).

Feeling lonely or misunderstood? That pair of black stilettos understands.

It's not unlike those who gamble to feel joy. You go into boutiques, and everyone is nice to you, and then boom! There's a sale on.

Look how much you saved! Of course, funds left your account. If you saved $50 but spent $100, you still spent $100 you were not otherwise planning to spend.

Shopping is not a bad thing. It keeps our economy running. If Americans don't shop, the terrorists win.

However, shop for what you need. Plan out shopping for things you want. Shopping can solve the problem of needing a new handbag, but it won't fix your self-esteem issues and the problems in your marriage.

With retail therapy, I don't care how cute the shoes are, your troubles will still be there, only next month, there will be the additional trouble of your credit card bills.

So before you decide that you need to run away from your troubles, realize that your troubles run a lot faster than you think they do. They'll catch up to you and bring some of their friends along.

Decide if you could better deal with your problems, be they worries over men, money or something in between, if you had a bigger butt, a headache or more bills. If any of those three options will help you, awesome, but I don't see how they could.

Otherwise, you are better off accepting what your worry is, moving on or taking steps to solve whatever the problem is.

Get professional help

I am not going to pretend I have never heard the words, "You should get professional help.".

Just like "professional help" can be a third-party voice of reason in a troubled relationship or a counselor in a time of crisis, "professional help," when it comes to money, can be that outsider looking in at what may seem to be a full-scale disaster.

Maybe it is a red-hot screaming emergency, one you don't realize the magnitude of, or maybe the mountain of horror you envision is really a molehill of "gee, I could do this a little better."

To make life livable, we each have to have a team because we can't do everything well. I've tried doing everything and have failed miserably. I now am all about teaming up with people who know what they are doing.

I used to think I could save money by cutting my own hair. And I did. For more than a decade.

And for those 10 years or so, my hair looked really bad. So one day, I decided that I really had no skills or talent whatsoever in the cutting of hair and added a stylist to my team. And sure enough, my bad hair days are few and far between.

We needed a new roof on the house. I recognize that the medical bills from me falling off the top of the house would cost more than hiring a roofer, with the plus of actually having a good roof. So I added a roofer to the team.

All of us need a team of professionals with some expertise we don't have. If I would do that with my hair and the roof of our house, why wouldn't I do that with my finances?

For years, too many, I have been more likely to hire a pro to trim my split ends than to make sure I was doing the right things financially. While my hair is something I look at every day, it doesn't control my future the way money does.

So here are some reasons why adding a financial professional to your team is a really good idea.

For starters, an advisor offers an objective opinion. That advisor will not melt into tears when looking at a bank statement and think that it means total and utter failure and decide to do nothing out of fear. That's what I have done a time or two, but I'm not a financial advisor.

Financial advisors should also not have a dog in the hunt. Some financial advisors do sell financial products or insurance, and that doesn't necessarily mean you shouldn't use them. After all, that may give them added expertise.

Some are paid by fees, but you pay a fee for that fabulous haircut. You need to decide if your financial planner's fees are worth the result of fabulous finances.

Others are paid by commissions on the products they sell. You can tell, though, when someone is more interested in selling you something than making sure you are making smart financial decisions. If something feels wrong, get another planner.

The way to find this out is to talk. Tell your potential financial advisor what your goals are. Do you want to retire early? Or retire at all? Or send your children to college? Toss all those dreams on the table.

Be honest. No hiding your disasters. I hired a housekeeper once, and then cleaned the house before she got there just so she wouldn't think I was a total slob.

You don't need to do this with your financial planner. No hiding your debts under the bed. Your advisor needs to know everything, so don't go to an advisor acting like you don't need one.

The whole point of having professional help is, oh, I don't know, getting professional help? Get what you pay for by being honest with your advisor about your situation as is and how you want to get there. Then your advisor can figure out either how to get you there or how to bring your champagne wishes and caviar dreams into what's actually possible.

You also need to find an advisor who is on the same page as you are. Are you cautious, or do you want to roll the dice and take some risks? Keep in mind, though, that your advisor may want to tell you to handle a few more risks or play it safe. Remember, you don't have all the answers, meaning that change may be needed. Calls for radical change, though, are a red flag that maybe your advisor isn't your financial success dream date.

Another red flag is urgency. Sure, you do need to save for your sweet babies' college education, but that doesn't mean you have to jump into an investment opportunity tomorrow, or for that matter, right this second. A good advisor will let you weigh your choices without making you feel rushed.

Stop worrying. Worry is a sign that something is wrong, but now you are doing something about it. Worry doesn't put money in your pocket, but learning, making better choices and acting upon them will.

Make sure you understand what's going on and where your money is going. A concept that can't be boiled down to a simple elevator speech or a few paragraphs isn't understood and needs either more simplification from your advisor or a pass from you. Finances can be confusing, so clarity is a must.

Get a to-do list and get it to-done. Your advisor can't do this alone. It would be like hiring a personal trainer to do your push-ups for you. You actually have to do the roll-up-your-sleeves work yourself. Your advisor is there to coach and advise, not make all the decisions and sign on all the dotted lines.

If you don't know where to start, go where the pros are. Hit the Certified Financial Planner website, cfp.net, for information, questions to ask and more.

The first step, and it sounds like a baby step but it is really one of those Neil Armstrong-type moves, is realizing that you are in charge. Not circumstances, your family, your ex, your boss or whoever you decide to add to your team as a financial advisor.

You are in charge, and you run your team.

Make learning more, working with those who can help you grow and making better decisions a part of your life, and you'll be where you want to be or an even better place.

Thrift shopping

A male friend and I came upon a gift of tickets to a ball, the Gentleman Friend and I.

But what to do?

It was black tie optional, and there wasn't a Fairy Godmother in sight. He didn't have a dark suit, and I was going to wear my go-to brown wrap dress. We would be going business dressy, or rather, underdressed.

"That's OK," I texted him. "The only one there I want to impress is you."

But good enough was not going to do.

Instead, he took me on a surprise treasure hunt the afternoon before the event. We were going to find our formalwear at the thrift shop.

For the uninitiated, thrift shopping can be either an exercise in feeling deprived or a grand safari where you stalk bargains instead of lions and elephants.

There was a time that nearly my entire wardrobe came from yard sales, thrift stores and the kindness of friends. These were days when demands were high and money was scarce, so I felt that anything beyond thrift store spending for myself would have been extravagant.

I can be a tightwad at times. I can pinch pennies and figure out ways to stretch a dollar until George hollers, but slowly I had crossed a line.

I had gone from trying to be thrifty to leaving myself feeling deprived.

Don't ever leave yourself feeling like this. It's not healthy.

Living richly doesn't necessarily mean spending money, lots of it or any of it. What it does mean is feeling like you are worthy.

You decide how you spend your money, but it is done with a sense of your worth and of doing the best not just for others but for yourself.

You realize that you are just as important as those you pinch pennies for.

Somehow, I had forgotten that fun should be included in every budget. That means that bargain-hunting can still be great fun, but it is a choice, not a must.

It means that if you see something you just love, a garment that would bring you joy with each and every wearing, that's your color and fits like a dream but isn't on sale, you should still get it.

Living richly means you are careful with your money but also are careful to enjoy it. After all, if you work hard for your paycheck, it ought to bring you at least one great-fitting pair of jeans.

After soul-searching, self care and counseling, I realized all this. And my spending became more about good choices, frugality with some fun included.

But back to our story.

We decided to find some ball-worthy duds, the deal being that we'd wear whatever we found.

There was a black suit coat for $3, a silk tie in vivid Mardi Gras colors and a crisp white dress shirt for him, and for me, a sheath of an evening gown, all black, with lace and sequins covering the bodice. It fit like it was made for me and was easily the most elegant piece of clothing I had ever worn.

A steal for $16.05 including sales tax.

It was the first time I felt like a princess wearing something from a thrift store, but I did. I couldn't have felt more Cinderella-like if I was wearing glass slippers and riding in a carriage that used to be a pumpkin.

We kept our deal, running off with our new purchases found after shopping like a couple of giggly teenagers. But we didn't merely wear our purchases to the ball, one of the most glamorous in the city.

No, we rocked them.

Whatever you wear, wherever you bought it, and for however much, rock it in grand style.

Sweaty T-shirts

Some people like to work out in "technical" shirts. Those are the ones that are silky to the touch and have tiny little holes in them to give you some air conditioning. And when you wear them, your sweat doesn't show. It just evaporates away.

And then there are people like me. I like a good old cotton T-shirt for working out.

Why?

Because the sweat shows.

It's stinky, not to mention unattractive, having great big sweat rings showing, and it pretty much repulses my children. If I have on a sweaty T-shirt, my daughter will leave the room until the offending garment is safely in the washer.

Why would I do this?

Because the hard work shows. I can leave the running trails with a sense of accomplishment, and I know that if I have stunk up the laundry basket and grossed out my family, then I got a good workout.

But then there is that saying about "never letting them see you sweat."

OK, apparently, I let the whole world see me sweat.

All the time. Like when I go to Wal-Mart and get so busy and let my head get so full of things to remember to do that I lose my car. That happens often enough that, in my family, I am known as "the Car Loser."

"Ma'am, have you forgotten where you parked your car?" a man driving by asked.

And, ashamed, I had to say yes.

And then there was a meeting at work.

It was at 3 p.m. I work as a features editor at a newspaper, and every day, there's some sort of deadline. It's like getting things done on time is a big deal there.

My department's deadline every day is 5 p.m. Clearly, this 3 p.m. meeting was going to mess with my afternoon.

The meeting dragged on.

I was learning next to nothing except that the "in conclusion" had passed by 30 minutes ago, and the presenter was keeping on keeping on.

I was getting antsy, and I am antsy by nature.

Here we were, well past 4 p.m. Less than an hour until deadline. When the meeting let out on the first floor, I was nearly sprinting to my computer on the second floor.

And next to me was my mentor, our publisher.

She was taking note, and not of the meeting.

About a week later, during a coaching session, I heard about it. What followed was some of the best advice, personal and professional, I have ever gotten.

"You know, Annie," she said. "You looked harried the other day."

It's OK to be harried, she said. Just don't look harried.

Being harried is contagious. If I was looking and acting like a woman about to lose her mind, it would send a signal to my team that they should be panicking.

Panicking people, she said, are not happy or productive.

And neither was I, when in panic mode. If you're going to lead, she said, you have to start by leading yourself.

Go scream in the ladies room, she said. Run around the block. Walk calmly to the parking lot, get in my car and holler. Cry in the broom closet.

Do whatever you need to do to feel better, but do not let the sweat show, she was telling me.

I related the exchange to my son, who sent me a box of relaxation herbal tea from his grad school digs in Memphis.

It gave me a smile, and I did enjoy brewing a mug in the afternoon. But what really helps you not lose your mind is all in your mind.

Not letting the sweat show, for me, means, at times, getting a handle on the mental panic that comes along with being late or nearly late.

That same sense of panic can come from feeling overwhelmed with responsibilities at work or at home or having a goal that you haven't gotten a bead on yet, let alone formulating a plan for reaching it. You're either running in 15 directions at once or frozen, and neither is good.

One strategy that works for me is not stacking my hurdles so high. If you know your to-do list is getting too long, instead of figuring out how you will do it all, figure out what can come off the list.

Is it vital that you yourself do it all? Are there jobs that can be delegated? Are there some things that really shouldn't be done or don't have to be done?

When you make your list, and you should have one, if only for the simple pleasure of scratching tasks off as they're done, be realistic. Don't make a day so full that you don't have a break. Don't leave yourself with no alternative to losing your mind in a hectic frenzy.

Be nice to yourself.

Give yourself time for breaks and de-stressing.

Make sure your life is in balance. I have noticed that when I tend to get the most stressed over situations, I haven't had enough water to drink, I haven't made time to think and pray and sit quietly, and I haven't gotten up from my desk for some outdoor exercise. Living an unbalanced life will leave you feeling unbalanced.

Another idea that's worked for me in hiding great big sweat rings is having a mantra of sorts. Feeling panicked because of a time crunch can be defused by me just taking a few slow, deep breaths and repeating in my mind, "I have all the time in the world. I have all the time in the world. I have all the time in the world."

This has been especially effective for me when driving. There have been times in the past when I was in such a knot over being somewhere on time that I was white-knuckle tense. I was leaning forward in my car seat as I drove in bumper-to-bumper traffic, as if that would somehow get me there faster.

That wasn't getting me to where I was going unless the destination was Stressville. It wasn't making me a better mother, employee or person. It was just putting me on the fast track to getting an ulcer.

Now, instead of continuing in a panic, I try to stop before one gets a toehold.

I've found that keeping my head keeps me calm. I get the work done or get to where I am going at the same speed, or with a steady un-frantic pace, faster, plus I feel happy and not hectic.

Happy feels a lot better, let me assure you. And when you are calm and happy and not looking overwhelmed, it tends to be a benefit to you personally and professionally.

Professionally, a calm and in control you looks like you've got it going on. Because you do.

And personally, let me ask you this. Do you want your sweet babies to remember you as being overwhelmed?

Do you want to always be able to make time for those you love?

Who's in charge here, anyway?

To not let the sweat show, you have to decide whether you are running your home or your home is running you. Are you running your career, or is you career running you?

Run your life, and run it at the speed that's comfortable for you and those you love.

Letting the figurative sweat show, as it turns out, may make you look like you are working hard for your money, but you won't look like you're working smart. You'll look busy, but not very effective.

Just like the literal sweat, it's not that attractive anywhere other than the gym or the running trail.

Thinking rich thoughts

I love to pinch pennies.

I like to think I can stretch a dollar far enough to make George Washington holler.

Making a box of hair color last two months instead of one, getting the last squeeze of toothpaste in the tube and the last few drops of body wash out of the bottle are almost like a game to some of us.

And there is nothing wrong with that, as long as you are not living with the mindset of want.

Making your dollars go farther should, at the end of the day, make you feel like you are not wasting. It should never make you feel like you don't have enough.

Anyone can have thoughts of not having enough. These thoughts have nothing to do with reality or the numbers on your bank statement. They have everything to do with your balances of faith and hope.

These thoughts, some experts on positive thinking say, will leave you poor.

I don't have proof to show that someone lost money, went from wealthy to broke, over thinking thoughts that they didn't have enough, needed to hoard every penny and would never measure up.

All I know is that thinking those thoughts is an unpleasant way to go though life.

I've had those thoughts and scrimped and trimmed to try to make ends meet during times when the family was, shall we say, underemployed. Nearly my entire wardrobe for work came from thrift stores, and I went a decade trimming my own hair instead of going to a professional stylist.

All I ended up with was a closet full of frumpy, ill-fitting clothes and a bad haircut.

Scrimping did not make our family wealthy. Most of the time, it didn't even make ends meet. Peter was still getting robbed so Paul could get paid.

It left me feeling poor in spirit, and when you are poor in spirit, you are poor indeed.

Because it costs nothing to have rich thoughts.

I am careful with our money. Sometimes.

I like to think that I scrimp on things that are worth scrimping on. I will change the family weeknight dinner menu based on what's on sale at Mac's Fresh Market, and I will comparison shop on everything from tissue to detergent. If I can get by with using less than directed of something and get nearly identical results, then I'm there.

But I will spend good money on running shoes.

I will buy jeans that only I have worn. I knew I was doing too much thrift shopping when it was like Christmas morning to get some clothes that were original to me.

And I will splurge on eating out with the family.

It used to be an everyday occurrence, eating dinner with my babies. But now, with two of them grown and living in different states, if I get at least three of the four in the same place, we're going to eat out and it will be a big tab.

If I want a glass of wine, I have it. I try not to mentally tabulate the cost before the check comes. And I don't gasp when I see the total.

Worrying never puts money in your pocket. If it did, rich thoughts would be rich reality. Worry only gives you wrinkles and ulcers. It robs you of any joy that might have been bubbling up today and does nothing toward your bottom line tomorrow.

If you're going to think thoughts, don't let them be thoughts that are consumed by worry. Let your thoughts be about the blessings you have now and the blessings you have to come.

You may not be able to afford a Jaguar, but do you really want one? I can look at one of those, think rich thoughts of not choosing to buy one of those instead of not being able to afford one and reap the difference of those statements. The first one is a statement of power, not poverty. I don't choose to buy one of those. The second is a statement of weakness and worry and things never changing for the better.

People who can afford Jaguars do worry about money, even though they have plenty. Those people are wealthy, but they aren't rich.

Rich people don't worry about their money. They don't spend it without a reason, and they don't waste it. They enjoy what they have. They spend where it counts, and they give some money away. They know that time is money, so they don't waste their time worrying about money or thinking thoughts of being miserly.

They may have money woes sometimes, but they face those with a plan instead of worrying over them.

Those living the rich life think thoughts of having plenty not of barely getting by. However much money they have, it is enjoyed down to the penny level.

Part III

Living Well and Taking a Few Bungee Jumps

Leaps of Faith

Never do you know a person's true self better than when you see them bungee jump.

If they're people of faith, they'll be praying and calling out to Jesus.

If the jumpers are people who pack along some F-bombs, they'll let a few go.

You'll find out where the line is between excitement and sheer terror for them.

At the Mississippi State Fair, they had a reverse bungee jump attraction. The thrill-seeker was strapped into a seat attached to a tall crane by a bungee cord that one hoped was good and strong.

The crane went up, the seat stayed on the ground and the cord stretched tighter and tighter. Knuckles turned white, eyes were shut and breath was held.

Then the seat was released from Mother Earth.

Just like a snapped rubber band, the bungee cord went this way and that, flinging the hometown daredevil here and there. Who knew where next?

Breath was no longer held. In an exhale of foul language and prayers, riders would holler for anyone who was listening.

After a while, words stopped. There was just a constant stream of whoops and screeches, joy and fear.

I'm not much for scary rides, but I've bungee jumped quite a few times in life.

We all have.

Did you decide on a career?

Did you get married?

Did you have children?

Have you been faced with being caregiver for a loved one?

Then you know a whole lot more about bungee jumping than those folks at the State Fair.

Sure, they went hurtling into the air with nothing but a bungee cord between them and horrific injury.

But when we take the leap of faith, we're jumping without a cord. No net, either.

It's just us and cold, hard reality.

And here is the terrifying part: there's no getting out of taking a leap of faith in life, because anything you decide is a leap.

Not jumping, not taking the risk, is just as much of a leap as leaping.

There are those who jumped at the chance of marriage early in life, and those who haven't married by midlife. Both are leaps of faith.

Have you weighed whether to accept a job offer? No matter what you decided, it was a jump, in this direction or that.

Deciding to be a parent is a leap of faith. Deciding not to be one is, too.

Life, as it turns out is one big leap of faith.

It doesn't matter whether you live life full-tilt or stay in bed with the covers over your head, you are making choices that have repercussions.

Who you are now, what you are doing, where you live, how much money is in your bank account and who you spend your time with are all results of decisions you've made and leaps you've taken.

You have been bungee jumping through life without even knowing it.

And through these decisions, in the terrifying moments and joyful times, the true you has shown through. There are the times we spew curse words and the times we pray quietly. Most of us do a little of both.

If life is a series of leaps, whether we tip-toe off the edge or run like maniacs before stretching our legs out to try soaring without wings, then why not embrace it?

Take the chances.

Dance, leap, jump and spin.

Gravity is there, and it works every time. That scares a lot of people away from leaping.

Just as those State Fair bungee jumpers went up toward the clouds, they went in the opposite direction, too.

What comes up must come down.

The reverse is also true. What comes down must come up.

Anyone who breathes, leaps, and anyone who leaps, stumbles and falls.

Leaps of faith are scary because they can't be taken back. You can't undo a bungee jump. Once your feet are off the ground, you go where you go, everywhere but backward.

But not leaping, not taking a few risks, can be risky, too.

Years ago, while taking a business class in risk management, I was part of a team of students writing a paper analyzing a situation. Our assignment was whether a family, let's call them the Joneses, should take a cruise to Hawaii.

We looked at the amount of money that vacation would have set them back. A pretty penny, to be sure.

What if they instead kept their money in the bank, or invested it in the stock market, or just used it to pay off some bills instead?

What if one of the Joneses gets sick on the trip?

What if, what if, what if.

Then we looked at the risk of not taking the flying leap.

They had the money, in our analysis, and the whole Jones family was going to go. Memories would be made. Fun would be had. Romance would be rekindled between Mr. and Mrs. Jones, making their marriage stronger. They'd go to luaus and hula dance and learn to surf.

Not going on the family cruise trip would be as big a risk as going.

The Jones family, in our estimation, should run to the edge and leap for all they were worth, landing with their feet on the deck of a cruise ship.

We jumped to that conclusion, and got an A for our efforts.

Bungee jumping is a terrifying thing, but so is life.

Take the leaps, and laugh and squeal, hoot and holler.

There's no if about falling. You will, not every time but sometimes. When you do fall, it probably will hurt.

But you have to take the leaps of faith and have faith. You have to take a few chances.

Being your true self means knowing the leaps worth taking. The decisions you make should line up with not only who you are now but who you want to be.

Face your fears and bungee jump your way through life.

Sure, you might miss the boat, but you might end up with great vacation videos from your cruise to Hawaii and memories of watching the sunset with your toes in the sand and a Mai Tai in your hand.

Jelly

"You are so jelly. You're peanut butter and jelly."

That's what my youngest daughter, says about being jealous.

While she and her middle-school friends laugh about being "jelly," it's actually not such a bad thing.

Grown women and middle-school girls all deny being jealous in situations. It seems petty and childish and embarrassing.

"I'm not jealous," we protest. And then go on to display all kinds of "jelly" behavior, fuming around, poor mouthing and generally not being happy campers.

"Jelly" doesn't seem that sweet.

Really, though, being jealous isn't something to deny. It's a natural reaction and one that can tell you about yourself and about those close to you.

A colleague gets the promotion at work. You think she's let it go to her head.

A friend loses 50 pounds. You think she looks fantastic but isn't as much fun to be around, you grouse.

Your cousin meets the man of her dreams. You're single and don't want to hear one more word about their happiness.

You're happy for them. Really, you are. You just wish you were in the same situation.

That's what jelly can show you.

Jealousy, while not usually considered to be a positive emotion, can become one if you use it to examine what it says about you, your thoughts and your dreams.

Thoughts about a colleague's success making her drunk on power may not have anything to do with your colleague's behavior. Instead, that jealousy may be telling you that you should be doing more with your own career.

True, your newly fit friend may not hit the all-you-can-eat pizza buffet the way she used to, but examine yourself to see if any negativity from you isn't instead a message from your own self to get in better shape.

Irritation over your in-love cousin may be a sign that you're hungering for a loving relationship in your own life.

No one wants to wish anything but the best for those they love, so instead of thinking ill of others who have great things going on in their lives, make some great things happen for yourself. If you do that, jealousy can be a sensor finding areas where you can realize personal improvement.

Of course, jealousy can also rear its green self in romantic relationships. And there are two reasons for that.

One is that the jealous party may have a serious lack of self esteem. There are those who can't trust that others won't betray them. There are men and women who will trail their respective significant others, thinking they will catch them in the act of some sort of philandering. And when there's no hanky-panky to be found, they're not convinced that their respective beloveds are faithful. They're convinced they just haven't caught them yet.

The other is because the person who's the subject of the jealousy isn't living up to commitments.

Jealousy can also be a personal alarm of sorts, too. It may be telling you that your significant other isn't living up to your expectations.

Let's not say he or she is running around. Let's say your expectations are mismatched.

And if you both have different expectations, say if one of you expects fidelity and the other is off sowing wild oats, then something has to change. Or someone.

The answer isn't doing what more than one friend of mine has done, becoming a P.I. of sorts, checking to see where his car is and trying to get passwords to his email and Facebook accounts.

It's not the answer because that is an unhappy existence. Who in her right mind would want to spend her time like that? Nobody who feels like she has to be a stalker can be happy.

Relationships should not make you want to do creepy things, and stalking someone is uber creepy.

If you can't trust someone, you can't be in a relationship with them, and that is true whether your jealousy is due to craziness on your part or is completely warranted.

Jealousy is unpleasant, but it is something you can learn from, even if the only lesson you take in is in the awfulness of it. Use it to learn and grow and not to be creepy.

Choose to be happy

When I get these children raised, then I will have fun and take some time for myself.

When I meet the man of my dreams, then I'll really enjoy life.

When these bills are paid, then I can be happy.

One day, we're going to laugh about our money troubles.

We've all said these and more. I can remember my Mama talking about how great Heaven was going to be and how life would be pain-free, trouble-free, worry-free and wrinkle-free there. There, she'd be happy and at peace.

I believe she was right. Heaven is indeed a place for joy. The problem is you have to die to get there.

Living well doesn't mean everything is going well. It means you choose to be happy in spite of your troubles, and make no mistake, we do have those.

I've had home repairs that made me feel like screaming, and on more than one occasion, I have declared that if Bob Vila was to show up on my doorstep, I'd marry him as long as he'd get to work on the laundry list of woes in this old house.

I let some rotten boards, cracks in masonry and a broken gate steal my joy. I had to remember back when I was renting and how thrilled I was to sign and sign and sign to own our family home.

Truth is, I love this place, and I am thankful for it. Not only that, but I am lucky to be here with a roof over our heads and a place to call home.

I remember thinking the bankers must have lost their minds, lending me enough money to buy a house, but 14 years and a few minor miracles later, I'm still making those payments like clockwork.

I'm grateful to make the payments and thankful for, among many things, that we have a family home, repairs and all.

That is where I had to find my happiness. It was hiding under that couch cushion called gratitude.

It's impossible to be unhappy yet thankful. Deciding to be happy and deciding to be grateful are pretty much the same thing. It's like buy-one-get-one-free on feelings.

Realizing how many blessings you have will leave you living a happy life this side of Heaven, and we all have some. Often, the things that are our greatest blessings can cause us the greatest amount of stress.

Such as children.

So many times, I have moaned and groaned over raising children. First, there's the sleep deprivation, then the demands and questions and tears and stitches and scraped knees. There are the bills and the schooling. There are messes and fender benders and broken curfews.

But I have been blessed four times. I could look at the hardships and complain about the unfairness of being a widow, listing all the struggles, but I would treasure the gift of being their mother.

Before my feet hit the floor in the morning, I am praying a prayer of thanksgiving for each of my sweet babies, thanking God in advance for all the blessings and protection he's going to lay on them that day. And He does.

Where you are now in life is a result of your choices, so why not choose to be happy?

So many times, I have worried over money and bills. Quite often, I have said out loud, sometimes to no one in particular, "One day, we're going to laugh about this."

Well, why can't one day be today?

Why wait for your problem to be fixed to let yourself laugh?

Add some joy and laughter to your day right now.

Laughter sure couldn't hurt. It's not like worrying was doing a whole lot for my bank balance.

Are you holding out for being in a loving relationship before you have some happiness? Being happy might attract the person you'll enjoy the rest of your life with, plus it's a lot of fun!

Be happy while you are raising your children. I don't know about you, but I want my children to remember their mama as happy. Overwhelmed and lonely does not make a good memory, the kind of memory I want my children to have.

Money won't make you happy, although plenty of us would like to test out that theory, just to be sure. Having more money might solve your money problems, but it won't fix your lack of joy.

Choosing happiness, it turns out, does have a price, and that cost is your worries, your ingratitude and your bad attitude.

If you are waiting for the absence of trouble before you enjoy life, you'll be in the sweet by and by before you get your joy. While Heaven's somewhere I'd like to go, I am in no hurry to get there.

I don't want to realize one day that I missed out on enjoying the happiness of each day by worrying over the next day, or how much there was to do or how much was in the checking account.

Choose to be happy.

Choose to count your blessings.

Choose gratitude.

And make those choices today.

Make your own happiness

I was at a dinner party one night, one with mostly women and just enough men to grill our dinner and then leave us to talk while they watched a football game.

And talk we did over glasses of wine, steak, asparagus and salad. When you get a few fortysomething-year-old women together over dinner and a cabernet, eventually we start trying to untangle all the world's problems, starting with our own lives.

A tangle indeed.

Eventually, the grass is greener on the other side of the fence. Not that we want to move next door. But we see things that our friends should be happy about but aren't.

Either that, or we have a "bless your heart" moment with a friend and just say, "Bless your heart" because she is a train wreck. Except that the train is carrying toxic, radioactive chemicals and is on fire and the tracks go off a cliff.

The woman across from me was miles from being a train wreck. She seemed to have it all. She was in her forties, but looked like a thirty-something.

She had large brown eyes and shiny, bouncing hair, and she rocked the pair of designer jeans she wore to our girls' night in. She enjoyed her job, and looked as healthy as can be.

Life should have been great for her. As my Dear Daughter would say, "She had it going on."

But life wasn't great for her on that evening.

"Why can't I just be happy?" she asked, her mood going from happy to miserable at the mention of men and love and marriage.

She wanted a relationship but in spite of being gorgeous and employed and otherwise fun at parties and not showing the slightest sign of wanting to turn a man into a purseholder, she didn't have one.

"I just want to be happy," she said, meaning happy with a man who loves her in a committed and caring relationship.

We single women do sometimes equate marriage with happiness, even those of us who have been married before and ought to know better.

Call it temporary amnesia. We forget that married life is not all sunshine, rainbows, glitter and unicorns.

And we forget that it doesn't bring us happiness.

Marriage may give us things to be happy about, but the kind of happiness that keeps us going when the car breaks down, the kids have the flu and there's a layoff round coming at the office is a do-it-yourself project.

You can't buy that kind of happiness, although some of us try.

And someone else can't give it to you, although some of us expect someone to.

The cabernet pretends it can, but it lies, in spite of its deliciousness.

No, that kind of happiness, the no-matter-what-happens happiness, the kind that keeps a shine on your stilettos even when the world's stomped all over them, that kind of joy we have to make ourselves.

It's a do-it-yourself project.

And although it sounds like a lot of work, and some days we feel like we can't find the instructions, we really should be making our own happiness.

One day, I was having a particularly rough time making my own happiness. I let my heart get all busted up over a man, and pretty soon I was in nobody-will-ever-want-me mode.

I was picturing myself alone, my children having moved away, with only my cats to keep me company, my weekend dates being named "Ben" and "Jerry," which would be better than "Jack," "Jim" and "Bud," but still.

My middle son had listened to me bellyache enough, and let me just stop right here and say this young man shouldn't have had to listen to this. Call it a moment of extreme weakness in mothering.

But he does exhibit wisdom beyond his years. And beyond my years.

"Mom," he said, "You are letting someone else be in charge of whether you are happy or not."

Oh. My.

My boy might as well be the oracle on top of Mount Olympus.

Ladies, how many of us are letting someone else or their actions determine whether we are happy?

How many? Too many.

Why is it we can have everything in order in our lives, only to be unhappy because the fact that we do indeed have it going on has not dawned on some man?

He may be a total idiot.

Letting a total idiot be in charge of your happiness is no way to go through life.

The first step in deciding to make your own batch of happiness is declaring that only you have the recipe for it, even if you can't find it or remember it at the moment.

Trust me. The recipe will come to you. You'll remember where you put it, or you'll just do what I do where recipes are concerned. Wing it.

The second step is counting the blessings you do have. Even the girl who's a flaming train wreck going off a cliff has something to be thankful for.

There was a hymn we used to sing at Calvary Baptist Church in West Point, Mississippi, and as a girl I thought it was a bouncy little ditty, as hymns go.

"Count your blessings, name them one by one. Count your blessings, see what God has done."

Well, ladies, start counting.

You didn't make it to adulthood on your own. Someone had to raise you. Do you have friends? Health? Vision? Do your legs work? Did you get an education? Do you have a job? A roof over your head? Sweet babies? Ice cream in the freezer?

There are all kinds of things to be thankful for if you take time to think about it.

And it is scientifically impossible to be unhappy while you are also being thankful. Try it. It's just like eating ice cream and being angry, another scientifically impossible feat.

Third, ladies, is not putting your life on hold while waiting for Mr. Right. And by the way, they don't tell us this in the storybooks, but sometimes Mr. Right's first name is "Always."

Life is a fleeting thing, and it is too precious to not be lived right now. So whatever it is that you are waiting on before you give yourself permission to be happy, assume it can catch up to you later. Because right now, you're busy hopping down the happy trail.

Think about how whatever you're seeking will make you feel. Using my friend's example, think about how you would feel if you were in a committed and joyful relationship.

Would it make you feel peaceful? Loved? Secure?

Whatever if would bring to you in the feelings department, just go ahead and feel those feelings now. Why wait?

And before you go ahead and email me that I have lost my mind, that I'm holding forth that being happy is that easy, I am here to tell you it is not.

Grief and loneliness, stress, money worries and a whole lot to do have tried their best to rob me of happiness. Plenty of days they succeeded.

Deciding to be happy is a lot of hard work. It's heavy lifting.

As a friend said to a grief support group I was in, "Fake it 'til you make it."

And some days, I do. Some days I have to will myself to look at the bright side, and when sad thoughts come, or worries, or stress, or negativity come to mind, I have to change the channel.

Immediately.

And there is no remote. I have to get off the recliner and change the channel my own self.

Making your own happiness means having faith that you're on your way but not there yet. It's willing yourself to think thoughts that work to your benefit.

Just like anything you practice, you become better at it as you go along. One day, you won't have to work at thinking positive thoughts quite so hard. And one day, you won't have to try.

You'll find that thinking thoughts to find happiness eventually will have happiness finding you.

Treat yourself well

Sometimes we women have to deal with a shrew of a woman.

She's mean.

She never once cuts you any slack.

You're never good enough, smart enough, pretty enough, thin enough. And she makes sure to let you know what she's thinking.

No matter what it is you're going to try, she's thinking you'll fail.

So who is this woman who's casting doubt on your dreams and calling you names you'd never allow your children to be called?

You see her every time you look in the mirror.

Ladies, we're kind to so many people. Even strangers on the street. We show care and affection to our children and partners, parents and siblings. Love is what makes us tick.

Why is it, then, with this enormous capacity for loving, that we can't be good to ourselves?

A video produced for a cereal company took women to a boutique for a shopping spree, only the tags of the clothing and signs on the displays read the same as the women were posting about themselves on the social media.

#thunderthighs.

Fat cow.

Gross.

I told you she was mean.

She's the one who whispers in your ear when you start daydreaming about furthering your education, writing a book or getting off the couch and training for a marathon.

"You're being silly."

"You're too old."

"Everyone will laugh at you."

"You'll fail."

When you see your reflection in the mirror or in a store window, no matter how beautiful you are, she's there to point out your flaws. All of them.

And she tells you that everyone else sees them, bigger than Dallas, even though in reality, everyone else is too obsessed with her own flaws to notice.

She's also keeping you in less than your best professionally and financially. She's the one who tells you you couldn't possibly go back to school because you're too old or would never pass. She tells you that promotion at work will never be in your reach and that you're not bright enough to learn about investing.

But here's something else about her.

She's a lying heifer.

All the meanness we tell ourselves, all the times we berate ourselves and our abilities, every time we see ourselves as less than we really are and less than we could be in the future, we're lying. Not just little lies, but whoppers.

The truth is that each of us is beautiful from the inside out, each of us is smart and can make wise choices, each of us deserves respect and each of us is worthy. But the only way any of us will be treated by others with the respect and dignity we deserve is to first treat ourselves with that level of respect and dignity.

To treat ourselves with respect and dignity means we first have to see ourselves as worthy of the best. Only then will we be to show ourselves the kindness we deserve.

To be kind to ourselves means we have to love ourselves.

For women, who show love and care to so many, this should come easier than it often does.

So many of us grew up reciting the Golden Rule, to love others as we love ourselves, yet if we actually did that, we'd be insulting, cruel and disrespectful to others, just as we are to ourselves.

Love ourselves first, and then we see ourselves as capable of more, as worthy and as lovable.

Respect follows, first by showing ourselves, our physical and emotional health and our finances respect, then by expecting to be treated with respect by colleagues and by those closest to us.

And those expectations are often met, merely because we see ourselves as worthy.

When those basic expectations for respect are not met, then changes have to occur. Maybe it's a job change. Maybe a relationship needs to end. Treating yourself with respect and kindness will require change, and change, even if it is only a change of mindset, is never easy.

Once you see yourself as worthy of respect, dignity and love, as worthy of a good life, a healthier lifestyle and smarter financial decisions will follow. Why? Because to live a good life, your best life, you need to be healed emotionally and treat your body and spirit with respect.

Money is a part of living the best life you can live. Money doesn't buy happiness, but it does buy housing and food. It pays tuition and determines how much work you need to do and where. Wise financial decisions determine your level of freedom and whether you will lose sleep at night worrying.

So, are you worthy of a good life, a life that is full and peaceful and happy?

If that's where you're wanting to go, the first step is loving the woman in the mirror.

The rest will follow.

Take care of yourself

"Take care of yourself."

Or sometimes, just "Take care."

It's a Southern way of saying goodbye. And also some really good advice.

Take care of yourself.

We're telling someone to care for themselves because we love them, or like them, or at least tolerate them. We want them to be safe and healthy and make good decisions. If they're cold, we want them to put on sweaters, and if they're hungry, we want them eating something healthy without spending too many Weight Watchers points.

"Take care of yourself" may be something we say off-hand, without thinking, sometimes.

But for a people who tell others, everyone from chance acquaintances to our children, "Take care of yourself," we're not very good at doing it when it comes to taking care of ourselves.

Taking care of ourselves is a true do-it-yourself project.

I've blamed all kinds of things and people for my own shortcomings in taking care of myself.

I've said I can't handle my finances because I'm no good in math. I've said I don't have time to exercise because I am too busy at work.

I've blamed stress for eating fast food, my family for me not making time for myself, and my bed for me not being able to get up early enough to have a moment of peace with my coffee and the Good Book before the day gets going.

None of those things are at fault. My bed did not conspire against me, nor did my family or my employer.

The truth is that I was not taking care of myself because I was not making it a priority.

Not one is going to take care of me – it's something I have to do.

Those who are married, don't hand that job of taking care of yourself off to your spouses. They may run errands for you, or cook your dinner or mow the lawn, but the job of taking care of yourself falls back to you.

It is your job to make sure you are getting enough sleep, making healthy choices, feeling happy and at peace, and yours alone.

Taking care of yourself is a DIY job, but it also has to be at the first of your list.

If taking care of yourself isn't your first priority, everyone and everything else in your life will be getting second best or worse.

I found out how important taking care of myself was after becoming a single parent. My husband of 18 years had died after a heart attack, and I was feeling overwhelmed, dealing with grief and raising four children and working full-time.

Facing that without taking care of myself was exhausting. And I had not been caring for myself.

One of the best pieces of advice I had ever received came to me then, just when I needed it most.

Treat yourself like a sick child.

What would you do for a sick child? You'd want that child to get plenty of rest, and you'd be kind to that child. You'd tell that child how precious she is. You wouldn't expect her to do everything at once, and you wouldn't berate her. You'd be patient and loving.

How many of you treat yourselves like a sick child?

Little by little, I started being kinder to myself. I stopped working late and found I had more energy for those I love. I started exercising, first with DVDs, then walking, then running, and found that I felt better. I started drinking more water, making better choices foodwise and doing some nice things for myself.

Simple things, like buying a new pair of jeans, painting my toenails or getting my hair trimmed.

Being happy is part of taking care of yourself. There was a time in my life when I thought the happiness of those I love was more important than my happiness, and that thinking otherwise would be selfish. I couldn't have been more wrong.

Happy people are happy. They are kind to others and have more energy. They're slow to anger and feel good, even great. Not only that, but they want all those around them to feel good, too.

Your happiness, the result of being kind to yourself and recognizing the blessings you already have, will bring happiness to all those you love, those you work with, and to everyone with whom you come in contact.

Taking care of yourself is far from selfish. It's one of the most unselfish things you can do, because you are giving the world a healthier you, a happier, more energetic, more productive you, a kinder, more caring you.

Why would you not want that for your spouse, for your babies, your friends, your coworkers, the checker at the supermarket and the person you pass on the street?

Butterfly effect

I like butterflies.

My favorite dress as a little bitty girl was a white polyester one printed with zillions of butterflies. I used to chase them in my yard, butterflies along with fireflies.

As insects go, butterflies are pretty lovable.

If you like butterflies, too, then hang in there with me as this essay is about the butterfly effect and how I think it can apply to your life.

According to the interwebs, the butterfly effect is a part of the chaos theory of mathematics. And yes, this could actually refer to personal checking accounts as well as meteorology, physics and economics.

Chaos theory studies the behavior of dynamical systems that are highly sensitive to initial conditions, according to wikipedia.

Did I just lose you?

In ordinary people speak, chaos theory holds that how things turn out later depends on how they start. Things that you do early on take effect.

The idea of the butterfly effect is that a hurricane's formation could hinge on whether a butterfly flapped its wings.

For us, those who are planning better futures no matter how far along life's road we are, it means that little things we do now can make a big difference later.

And who doesn't like the idea of thinking about ourselves as butterflies? They're gorgeous as insects go. They're probably the only insect you don't want to fry with a bug zapper or send to their eternal reward with a plastic swatter.

And they start out as sort of blah-looking caterpillar that then goes into a bug dressing room and has a big make-over reveal. What's not fabulous there?

So, my butterfly friends, let's get to flapping those wings, and maybe we can brew up a hurricane.

Metaphorically. No real-life Katrinas, Betsys or Camilles. Think of it as the drink they serve at Pat O'Brien's, which is pretty yummy and potent.

Ahhh. Here's to a more yummy and potent future with no wind damage.

The thing that's so butterfly-tastic about this idea is that little changes are easy. Baby steps.

Over the years, when I have tried to reform myself, I've been an all-or-nothing kind of girl. I say I am going to balance my checkbook to the penny each day or start every morning with an hour of lung-busting cardio or swear off everything that tastes good, and I'm great the first day. Maybe even the first week.

But then I fall off the wagon with a check bounced on a purchase of a box of Ding Dongs devoured during the time I set aside for exercise. Call that a bad day.

Then it is like the whole year is wrecked because of a bad day, and I go back to being me, imperfections and all.

Looking at yourself as the butterfly part of the butterfly effect doesn't mean you turn out perfect, by the way. We all slip up.

What it does mean is that we pick something we'd like to improve and flap a little here and there, getting a little better as time goes by. When we slip up, we just start over the next day, flapping our little butterfly wings a little.

Thinking about change as a butterfly effect also works well because change is not only hard to stick to, but also hard to start.

You'd think we'd be in a hurry to make changes that would result in better lives down the road, and you'd be wrong.

If it was easy to save more money, lose weight, get in shape, get out of debt, find the love of your life or put yourself or your sweet babies through college, everyone would be happy, healthy, debt-free millionaires with Ph.Ds. And you just don't see one of those every day.

It may not be easy each day, but flap those beautiful butterfly wings. You'll be soaring before you know it.

Time management

My time as a manager has put me either in front of Power Point screen or behind a book or two on time management.

It sounds good, doesn't it?

Time management.

The thing is, it's not the time that needs management. Time does just fine on its own.

We're the ones who need the managing.

What can seem like a lack of time in reality is a lack of priorities and direction.

Women, you know we have a special relationship to time. Apparently, judging by the activities of myself and my cohorts, we think we can multitask to the point of quantum leaping into a parallel universe and multitasking there, too.

You know, so we can be multitasking while we're multitasking.

Somehow, becoming mothers only amplifies this. We can do pretty much anything from cooking a dinner to running a company one-handed and with a baby on the hip.

But plenty of times, we think about things we want to do or be, things that would help us in the long run, and what do we do?

"I would love to do that," we say, "but I just don't have time"

Or "I'm too old to go back to school."

And this is why we're the ones who need the managing.

Time, after all, does what it is supposed to do. It passes. It fugits, it flies, it flows like a river.

We're the ones who stall out and get stuck.

We all get 24 hours in a day. Every day. No one gets 25 or 26. And we can spend those 24 hours however we'd like.

Those last three words are key. However. We'd. Like.

In other words, we can spend them according to our personal priorities.

If we know we should exercise but can't find the time, what that really means is that we'd rather sleep an extra hour or watch TV on the sofa than be healthier.

Got a special dream? Writing a book or starting your own business? What are you doing now that you'd trade to do something that would result in your life being better tomorrow than it was yesterday?

It's not easy. Spending that time wisely might mean missing some TV time or getting up early or changing habits.

But if sitting on the sofa eating potato chips would give you an awesome life, then what awesome lives we all would have.

Just like we need to spend our money carefully, we have to spend our time carefully. Even more so.

Because you can always find a way to make more money, but try as you might, you have those same 24 hours every day. Time goes away, and you can't get it back. The past is spent, the future is like credit card spending, not really yours yet, and all you really have is now.

Which brings me to the idea of being too old to do something, or if you start, you'll be too old to enjoy the results. That is just stupid—and I have said those very things about myself.

Time is going to pass by anyhow. Do you want to be five years older and still stuck or five years older and with a book or two under your belt or a degree in hand?

Spending time might be the wrong terminology. What we really need to be doing to create a more prosperous future is investing our time. Spending our time where it will pay off in the future.

We all know that quality time with the sofa and chips will only pay off with time needed in the gym.

Spend the time you need to learn about managing your finances or paying down debt or investing. Invest the time needed to start that business that would improve your bottom line while giving you more time with those you love.

Want to run a marathon? Improve your health and well-being?

Or maybe you want to write the novel you've been tossing around in your head. Or earn a master's degree or start a new career or renovate your house.

Manage how you spend the minutes and the hours. That's where most of the spare time is.

Listen to audio books during your commute. Bring your textbooks to your kids' soccer practice. Get up 30 minutes earlier. Skip 30 minutes of TV.

The other trick is to do this regularly. Make good use of little bits of time and you'll end up with the sum of time invested being greater than its little 30-minute parts.

Let time manage itself, because it will anyway. It does its thing, sunrise to sunset.

Instead spend your efforts managing yourself.

It will be the best investment of time you ever make.

I'm rubber, you're glue

On the playground, when things got ugly, we used to say the little rhyme, "I'm rubber, you're glue. What you say bounces off me and sticks to you."

There's a lot of truth to that little poem, trotted out whenever one kid insulted another.

The words we say and the thoughts we think do stick to us rather than the one we aim them at. This is why there's another rhyme, in the form of a prayer, that goes, "Oh, Lord, may the words I say be soft and sweet, because they may be the words I eat."

I'm rubber and you're glue. What you say bounces off me and sticks to you.

Let's flip that, because if I am glue, then everything I say sticks to me.

Everything you say sticks to you.

If we're all walking around with our words stuck to us, then they should be really good words.

Kind words.

Pretty words.

Happy words.

It's been said that what people say about others says more about them than the people they're talking about. It's also been said that whatever you lob at others wordwise lands on you.

If that's true, and they're rubber and you're glue, and what you say bounces off them and sticks to you, then speak words of blessing and encouragement.

Speak those sweet words over yourself, and over your children, to those you love and over your job.

We've all been on diets, but this one will taste like soft, sweet words instead of celery sticks and SlimFast.

Try going a week without negativity, without insults, spoken or thought, about yourself or others.

Instead of thinking about hardships, dwell on the positive and the possible.

Don't think of what you don't want. Instead, think about what you do want.

Don't think, "I don't want to be lonely," or "I won't ever get these bills paid." Think thoughts of all you have to offer, all the blessings you do have and how things are only getting better. What you resist will persist. If you resist loneliness, you will stay lonely. If you look at the many blessings in your life, then you will have more of them. So many you'll forget all about being lonely.

Some might call this sugar-coating reality.

But reality goes down a whole lot easier that way.

Sugar-coated reality, spoken and thought of often enough, has a funny habit of becoming just plain old reality.

Even if it doesn't, isn't it a whole lot easier, and more pleasant to think the good thoughts and say the words of blessing and encouragement?

Bits and pieces

Sometimes you look at what has to be done, how much time it will take, how much work it will be, you're just stunned into doing nothing.

I've done that, battled that, got the T-shirt and Instagrammed the photos.

I can be such an all-or-nothing kind of girl. I think I have to finish what I start, so I can scratch it off my to-do list.

I vow Jan.1 to exercise for an hour a day, miss a day, and fall off the wagon and onto the sofa.

I decide that there's no way I can clean the house in the time I have, so it is all or nothing. I don't take a lick at the snake, as the old saying goes. I just let it slither around and be a snake, not swatting at it because I think it might take a while to kill it. Either the house will be a train wreck or clean.

Those are just minor examples. If I can do that with little things like working out and housecleaning, imagine what I can do with dreams and goals.

There's no way I can go back to school to earn a master's degree with children at home. Plus I'm over 40. I'm too old.

I can't write a book. I don't have time, between raising children and working full time.

It's quite amazing how I have found myself rooting against being in shape, having a clean house and a master's degree on the wall.

True, it does take time to write a book. Or to earn a degree, start a business, train to run a marathon or whatever it is that has you dreaming.

I am not made of time. Yet somehow, I did find time in the past five years to finish a master's degree and to write a book.

Housecleaning has been lower on my list of priorities.

How did I do it? I used up the bits and pieces of time. These are all over the place. They're in the getting up 30 minutes early and in the wait at the car repair center and your kid's soccer practice. A bit of time at lunch to study there, and a little staying up late or getting up early there.

It's not easy, of course, but pursuing a dream is worth rolling out of bed a little early. Finishing the writing of a book does feel better than staying in a warm bed. Even in January.

One reason for using those bits and pieces is that, just as sand fits around big rocks, they fit around the boulders in our lives. You know, the big things like being a good parent or a significant other worth having or taking care of your health, body and spirit.

After all, what good is reaching your goal if it comes at the cost of letting your relationships languish or becoming unhealthy and stressed?

I was bemoaning that I had less time to spend out on the running trails while writing a book in my bits and pieces of time. My daughter said, "Which do you want to be, in shape or finishing your book?"

That's an excellent question, since life is all about choosing between this and that. But some things you should never choose between.

"I want both," I said. And I do. Actually, I want it all.

I want time for being healthy and at peace, close relationships with my children, time for fun with my friends and a Gentleman Friend who thinks he's the luckiest, most spoiled man in the world. Oh, and a career as a writer and editor with a few books to my name.

That's not too much to ask, is it?

Pinch off the suckers

If you have ever grown tomatoes in the back yard, then you might know what I am about to reference.

Suckers.

A sucker is the little sprout of a branch that grows between the main stem of a tomato plant and a larger branch.

A sucker looks good. They are usually green and leafy if you let them get a toehold, but it's really not a good idea to give a sucker a toehold.

Why pinch off a branch that looks green and leafy and makes the tomato plant looks more full and lush?

Well, it depends. Keep the suckers if you want a green tomato plant. Pinch off the suckers if you want tomatoes.

You see, those little suckers are aptly named. They suck nutrients away from the production of tomatoes and put it toward making a bushy tomato plant that doesn't produce as many tomatoes.

Pinching suckers off is not hard. You find them and break them off the vine, one at a time, taking in the aroma of tomato plants. Like newspaper ink and new tires, tomato plants have a scent that you wouldn't think you'd like, but you'd be wrong. To me, tomato plants smell like summertime.

You do want to pinch them off, though, so pinch, pinch, pinch. Because growing tomatoes should be about growing tomatoes.

Tomato plants aren't the only place you will find suckers. They are all over the place. They are the people in your life who suck all the joy and energy out of you, leaving you too drained from their drama to be productive and fruitful.

Suckers are activities that are not beneficial. They are the Candy Crush Sagas and Farmvilles when you ought to be working. They suck away time and leave you with no fruit for your trouble.

Suckers are bad habits.

Suckers can make nothing out of something.

Your sucker might be your sofa and the remote control.

It might be a habit that steals your joy or your health.

It might be working hard but not smart, letting long hours suck all your energy away.

Your sucker might be neglecting yourself, robbing yourself of sleep, good nutrition, relaxation, healthy exercise and time with friends.

Leaving you with no fruit in sight.

What are you growing?

The Bible calls the "fruit of the spirit" love, joy, peace, patience, kindness, goodness, faithfulness, gentleness and self control.

Fruit can also be your goals or the fruits of your labors. Fruits are your results, what you want to harvest.

Before you start pinching off your suckers, you need to decide what kind of fruit you want to grow.

Just what do you want, anyway?

Do you want to improve your health? Run a marathon? Finish your college degree? Get a better job? Save your marriage or, for you singles, meet the man of your dreams?

Do a little daydreaming. And write it all down, just in case you forget. Get as detailed as you dare. What does being fruitful look like to you?

Then figure out what you need to do to get there. How do you get there? What path do you take?

Figure out your path, or at least a few steps in the right direction. If you want to improve your health, then maybe the first step is taking a mile-long walk each day. If you want to finish that degree, maybe your first step is exploring what programs are available online or in the evenings or weekends.

You now have your main stem – your dream, your faith and your hope – and a branch, those first small but positive, powerful steps in the right fruit-bearing direction.

What's keeping you from taking those steps?

Figure out what is robbing time and energy away from you and being fruitful. How is it sucking away your energy and stealing your future? When and where?

Then be ruthless. Pinch with abandon.

Pinch off the suckers, one by one, day by day.

It may be a little uncomfortable at first, but pinching off habits usually is. It may be getting up sleepy at 5 a.m. to study for that college class or write that great American novel, or getting tired and sweaty from putting in the miles on the running trail, or having to get used to more green veggies or less caffeine, more crunches and fewer Nestle Crunches.

What you will find is that, without the suckers, you will have more life, more energy, and get ready for a harvest, because you can't help but be fruitful.

Codependence Day

There should be a holiday called Codependence Day. Everyone could try to fix each other's lives, blame their bad decisions on other people and be miserable while shooting off fireworks and grilling hotdogs.

I have been called codependent by a trained counselor, so, in Southern speak, I can talk about them.

Years ago, I went to counseling. Admitting that I needed help was one of the hardest things I ever did, but also one of the best gifts I could have given myself. I wanted some tips on how to live with my husband without losing my mind, and I thought the counseling session was going to be an hour-long session of me telling the counselor about all the things I had to put up with. Because I was the one without problems, you know, Little Miss Perfect.

Let's pause here to laugh about the ridiculousness of this thought.

No, the counselor said, we're going to talk about *your* problems.

"What?" said the woman who drove herself to the counselor's office. "I don't have any problems."

I was the one who held down a job, got the little people to school, cared for my parents. My problem was that I didn't have a Presidential Medal of Honor and a halo floating over my head for all these heroics.

After the counselor figured out that I was not hearing voices or exhibiting multiple personalities, she said, "I think you may be codependent."

I was insulted. Miss Goody Two Shoes was not one to have issues.

The counselor wrote down the title of a book and recommended that I read it and come back to tell her if I was codependent.

So, of course, Miss Rule Follower read the book in between taking on the happiness of my family as my own responsibility and surreptitiously fixing any problem anyone in my home had. And lo and behold, yes, I agreed. I think somewhere in the first 10 pages.

Codependency, like the road to hell, is paved with good intentions. You love someone so you want them to be happy. And there is nothing wrong with that unless you think that their lack of happiness, career problems and health are somehow your responsibility.

Somehow, in my twisted little mind, I figured that any lack in the lives of my family was my bad. If I was a better woman, my husband would be a better man and my family would live a life that was a blur from one joy-filled day to the next. And that was where I crossed the line.

I was an enabler, doing the worst thing I could when all I wanted was to do the best.

I wanted happiness for those I loved, and instead I made myself miserable, along with everyone else in the house.

Here's the deal: All these movie lines about how happy they make each other, the "You complete me" lines, are just made up by screenwriters. They don't work in real life, because in real life, it is not healthy to walk around incomplete.

I don't know about Renee Zellweger, but as for me, I want a whole man and whole friends, and not pieces and parts of anything. But more than that, I personally don't want to be a fraction. Not only do my whole man and whole BFFs deserve a whole me, but I do.

I complete me by my own self.

It's your job to go complete yourself.

Everyone is in charge of his or her own happiness. It can't be given to you by anyone else, and try as you might, you can't give it to anyone else. Which is good if you think about it.

If your happiness can be given to you, it can also be taken away. But if you make your own happiness, you can have a never-ending supply. And that would be something worth celebrating with hotdogs and fireworks every day.

The blessing of being blessed

My husband had recently passed on, and while we were getting by on a day-by-day basis, we were, in fact, getting by. Bills got paid, dinner got made.

You'd rather take a beating than ask for help, a friend once said to me. That's actually not quite true, as I'll pass on the fisticuffs, but asking for help has always been a little difficult for me.

Let's call it an acquired skill.

I had tended to figure that everybody has enough to say grace over just getting through life without having me add to their plate.

I was a grown woman, and grown women handle their own problems.

But all my independence ran headlong into my church friends. A dear church friend now departed used to say that there are no friends like your church friends, and he was right. Church friends, upon hearing of a death or illness in the family, will show up on your doorstep with casseroles within the hour.

If faith without works is dead, let's just say their faith is good and lively. Your church friends are just not going to be at peace unless they're helping in your time of need. And you won't be, either.

So here I was, trying to bring home the bacon and fry it up in a pan, trying to prove that I had it all together and didn't need any help, and my phone starts ringing.

It was my church friends. The United Methodist Men. They wanted to go build something or fix something, but I couldn't think of a thing that needed building or fixing.

So I politely declined a few times.

Then I got a call from one of the wives of the United Methodist Men.

"Really, we are fine," I told her.

"I know you're fine, but you need to let them do something," she said. "Do that for them."

So when they called again, I told them I had a gate that needed fixing. And then one of the United Methodist Men came up with the idea of building my children a sandbox. And I said that having a sandbox for them would be lovely.

The United Methodist Men brightened up. They had a purpose, a mission. And they showed up bright and early with tool belts on, just grinning. Nobody is happier than a church men's club member with a project.

By noon, I had a working gate and a sandbox. And a lesson. When someone offers you a blessing, offer them a blessing back by accepting it.

"I don't need your help" is not the right response. "Thank you" is.

Sometimes, others need to help you as much as you need to accept it. The blessing, then, comes to you both, and both the giving and the accepting are good for the soul.

It is a blessing to let someone bless you. For them and for you. For them, they get the feeling of making a difference because they are making a difference. For the receiver, the blessing is admitting that you do need help and that you can't do it all on your own.

That doesn't always come easily, admitting you need help and accepting it. But doing so is like exhaling. Doing it all means carrying it all on your own, and that is one heavy, stressful load.

Carrying it all is a lot of baggage. Blessing someone by letting them bless you by helping tote the load makes the journey easier for you both.

Give them something to talk about

Call it a byproduct of living in a small town.

People talk about each other. They say in small towns, people know what you're going to do, and talk about it before you do it, and they're right.

Talking about other people can be the most interesting thing going on, if you're in a small place.

My own sweet mama cared a great deal about what other people thought and said. She did a lot of worrying about it, too. Many of the times I got in trouble as a girl, the lecture turned to "What will people think?"

This took up quite a bit of her time, thinking about what other people thought, and she was a Bible-reading Sunday school teacher whose strongest drink was coffee.

If they were thinking and talking about her, I don't know what they could invent to make scandal, but trust me, they'd have to invent something. Mama was a sweet woman whose worst fault was worrying too much about the opinions of others.

She wasn't alone in this. I have also worried about what others would think from time to time, and I think we all have.

Guess what.

Those people we worry about, wondering what they're thinking about us? They're busy worrying about what we think about them.

It's true.

We worry over what people think, and most of the time, they're not thinking about us at all.

They're in their own little worlds, thinking about anything from whether they cut the Crock Pot on before they left for work or how they're going get everything done by the time it's supposed to be done. Who knows what they are thinking about, but it's pretty likely it's not us.

Most people just don't have time to think critically of others. That's most people, though.

There are some who will not only think about others, but talk about them. And they're not bantering about how pretty and sweet others are.

In high school, they are the mean girls.

Some mean girls never graduated. Same goes for their male counterparts. They populate business offices, churches, hometown country clubs and neighborhoods.

And they do talk about you and me.

How do I know this?

Because we have all heard them talking about others. When you leave the room, you're the next topic of conversation.

I know, you're probably thinking that by writing about people whose focus is talking and tsk-tsking about what other people are doing, I am doing the same as they are, only I inserted it in a book.

The answer is no. It's not the same thing, because they are not my focus in life. This essay is not about those who speak in a toxic way about others but about dealing with them.

I don't base my self worth on criticizing others to make myself look better in comparison, and you shouldn't either.

We should all be so busy living our own lives that we don't have time to dwell on what others should be doing.

Don't use the excuse, "But, Annie, we're just talking about them so we can be in prayer for them."

Don't announce at your women's prayer circle that "we should all be in prayer for Peggy Sue, who I saw walking into the liquor store in that short dress. You know she's got a drinking problem."

Pray for her, sure. Just don't broadcast it.

The choreographer and dancer Martha Graham is credited with saying, "What people in the world think of you is really none of your business."

I wish I had said it.

It's true. Graham could think as well as she could dance.

What other people think, or say, about us is really none of our business. What other people think about and say also says a lot more about them than it does about us.

So let them think or talk.

Everyone's got an opinion, and not all of them are going to be ones you agree with or ones that are flattering to you. In fact those who do anything in life, attempting a bungee jump to some audacious goal, are going to be a topic of discussion, so if you're going to take some leaps, you might as well get used to it.

One of my friends back home used to say that unless something would matter in 100 years, it wasn't worth worrying about. What others think definitely falls into that category.

If you can't say anything nice, don't say anything at all. That's the way the old saying goes. Think good thoughts, and speak encouragement. It may make others have a better day, but it will definitely improve your mood.

Some folks are going to talk no matter what you do, so you might as well give them something to talk about.

Live life fully. Take a few risks. Be silly and sometimes ridiculous.

Keep your faith, and don't let your heart and soul go unexamined.

Live and leap for all you're worth.

Predict the future
(by creating it)

There have been so many times in my life when I wished for a crystal ball. Not just the old Magic 8 Ball I'd quiz as a child, but a real, honest-to-goodness fortune-telling crystal ball.

Living out the future a minute at a time isn't enough for me. I've always been a planner, and plans are so much more accurate when you know what's going to happen.

I've chosen career paths and wished for a sign that I was on the road to, if not fortune, just having a bit more money at the end of the month.

First dates have had me wishing for some sort of psychic knowledge as to whether this was Prince Charming or just an old toad. Just so I could plan my social life accordingly.

I've wished I could see ahead to keep my parents well and my children out of trouble, to keep my house repaired and to make sure I had a retirement worth retiring to. It seems like the word "alas" would go well here. Because you know how this is going to end.

Alas.

I have yet to find some good, dependable, working fortune-telling gadget. Not even on late-night TV infomercials.

I think the psychics with the hotlines tend to make it up as they go along. I haven't called one so perhaps I am being unfair, but if I were going to call a psychic and pay by the minute, then I would be more apt to stay on that line if I was hearing nothing but sunshine, rainbows, unicorns and glitter.

So that's going to taint things a little.

I figure that the only way I can get a handle on the future, financial, personal, professional and what have you, is to create it.

The best way to know the future is to make it myself.

Granted, we're all subject to fate, and I will be the first to admit I can't completely create the future.

If I could, then don't you think my lifestyle would be a little bit more upscale?

If I were in the future-creating business and were that good at it, don't you think that I'd have a few unicorns playing in the backyard?

This wasn't exactly the future I'd have picked off the store shelf, but I can cope. And I can make smart decisions that actually can help create a better future.

One thing I can do is stop doing stupid things. That always makes the next day a little easier to deal with.

If I don't eat an entire box of Ding Dongs today, then I won't have to chain myself to the Stairmaster tomorrow.

If I hang out with losers and users today, nothing good will come of it tomorrow.

If I don't whip out the plastic every time something catches my eye, then I won't have a huge bill with high interest later.

Another thing I can do is start doing smart things. It's like planting a crop – if I plant apple seeds, I won't get avocados. If I do the smart things early, then there should be a good future later, or at least the odds are improved. And I want to grow a bumper crop of great things happening.

If I study what investments would make sense for my 401(k) today and acted accordingly, then I might have a little nest egg when I get ready to retire instead of having to wonder if Wal-Mart would hire me as a greeter.

If I think good thoughts and read inspirational books today, my outlook will be better tomorrow.

If I make a point to walk at least a mile each day, then I'll be healthier tomorrow. Ditto on drinking more water and eating more fruits and veggies and finding a slice of peace and quiet at some point in the day.

If I work on enjoying a rich and full life, on being the kind of partner worth having, on making sure I am in a good place emotionally, then my chances of being in a healthy relationship in the future are better. At least I would have a better chance of at least knowing what a healthy relationship looks like when one comes along.

If I make it a habit to develop my skills professionally, then the chances of me continuing to be employed are greater. And even if, in this rocky economic terrain, I was to find myself having to launch a job search, it would increase the chances of me finding another job, and perhaps a better one.

Act instead of react, or worse, just lying there like a lump while life comes at you like a Mack Truck.

Take the steps to be who you'd like to be, to live the kind of life you want to live, and you won't even need any fortune-telling devices. You'll be the one with the answers instead of that Magic 8 Ball.

Afraid to fail, afraid to succeed

Fear is an odd thing.

We think we only fear the negative and the scary. Bad things. Nightmares. Boogie men and not just the ones who wear white polyester disco suits.

In reality, though, what we often fear is change.

We don't want to leave the comfort zone.

After all, it's not called the comfort zone for nothing. It's La-Z-Boy recliner comfortable.

Change is not comfortable. It's difficult and feels awkward, and that's change such as marrying or becoming a parent, changes we view as joyful.

Other changes, such as having to change careers after being laid off, having to lose weight or exercise after a come-to-Jesus talk from your doctor or adjusting to life after loss, don't have the sugar-coating of joy to make them easier.

Those are just hard.

We didn't choose those changes, and we're not happy about having to make them.

We're afraid to fail, on one hand. Making positive changes in your life does bring with it the chance of failing. Make that leap, and maybe the bungee cord snaps.

Failing doesn't mean that others will roll their eyes at you and laugh, although they might. It means you will have to dust yourself off after a leap of faith and a fall.

That's the hard part, and that's what we fear.

Not trying to change has no failure risk to it. No effort gets wasted, and you can't fault someone for failing when they don't even try.

That scenario doesn't feel risky. The problem is that this comfy, no-change area has the much larger risk of not only making no progress but backsliding.

Nature rarely ever lets someone or something stay the same. Change is constant in our world and in ourselves. So you can either change by heading downhill, or up. There are fears that on the surface don't seem to make sense, such as the fear of going uphill instead of down.

Many, if not most of us, fear success just as much as we fear failure, and perhaps more.

Success can seem like something near euphoria, but success also means change. Reaching your goals is also not nearly as familiar as failure, since, as humans, we fail all the time. We're used to failing, so it may feel more comfortable than succeeding.

Success leaves you with questions.

What if success at work means your friends in the break room won't be as comfortable hanging out with you at lunch? A meaningful relationship could change how much time you have for friends, family or yourself.

Losing weight would be wonderful for your health and self image, but it will mean creating a new comfort zone that doesn't revolve as much around food. You might fear that those you used to eat pizza and drink beer with won't like the new, healthier you, or at least won't find the new you to be as much fun.

These fears, whether acknowledged or not, will leave you smoking when you need to quit, overweight when you need to lose, earning less than you should and stuck in whatever rut you're in.

Fear of taking whatever chance you need to take to reach your goals or make your life better can paralyze you from making a move or taking a chance.

Fearing both success and failure can leave you stuck in your comfort zone, and let me tell you, nothing good ever happens there.

There's also the fear of what other people will think. I grew up in a small town, and anyone who grew up where most people knew each other and got into each other's business will tell you that what other people think can be a concern.

Don't let it be.

Success can make you stand out. The spotlight can be unnerving. Sitting off behind the scenes is easy. Nobody ever talks about you critically if you can't be seen and aren't doing anything worth talking about.

Besides, people will always talk about something. Might as well give them something good to discuss.

Success may mean you have some people who, out of jealousy, aren't your friends anymore. Guess what? They never were to start with. Your real friends will cheer you on when you succeed and dust you off when you don't.

The life you want to live, the life you should live, is going to mean taking some chances, standing in the spotlight sometimes and taking a fall others.

Face your fears and take your leap of faith. Failures teach you, and success shouldn't be scary. Staying in the recliner-like comfort zone too long, though, is a true fright. Besides, I just know that the seats in our individual comfort zones probably have spills on the chair arms and potato chip crumbs where the cushions meet. It's nowhere you want to stay.

Wake up already

Used to be, happiness meant lolling around in bed, the later the better.

I was a teenager then, and Saturday mornings, and weekday mornings in the summertime, used to mean getting up about noon. Then generally nothing healthy or productive happened until afternoon, if at all.

Later on, there was college, including 8 a.m. classes and work, and I managed to haul myself to both, waking up at the latest possible time to allow for maximum lolling time while still moussing and blow-drying my hair. Remember, this was in the 1980s.

Then there was marriage and motherhood, but I still kept that habit of wanting to stay in that bed.

The times I slept with an electric blanket, I'd cut it off and loll some more in bed as to not waste electric blanket heat. You know, just to be environmentally friendly and not waste electricity.

I'd loll if the kids crawled in bed with me and blame my lolling on them.

They eventually got to be school-aged, and I'd get them to school. Looking like a train wreck. Then I'd be at the office, a little sleepy still and more than a little rough around the edges.

Then I had an epiphany.

I had started getting up earlier, first because I took up running. Only people with rabid wild animals chasing them run past 9 a.m. in the summer.

Then I had some morning planning sessions for my features editor gig at the newspaper, so I traded those for morning runs and pushed exercise to the evenings or weekends.

When I started writing my first book, "Because I Said So: Life in The Mom Zone," I knew there was no wiggle room in my schedule. I didn't want to write a book about being a mom while I was taking time away from my children. That would have landed us all in counseling.

And there was the day job at the newspaper, one I love and one that pays regular. The only place to get some writing time was early.

You do what you've got to do.

I set my alarm for 5:30. I'm not going to lie—it was awful leaving my bed.

Awful. But a pot of coffee brewing would knock the cobwebs off my brain, and I'd write. Then I realized I also had time to read a little, and eat breakfast, and get in the bathroom before my children start hogging the mirror and sink.

By the time I was waking up children for school, I was dressed with some lipstick on and my hair brushed. I was awake and in a happy mood.

And who doesn't want to wake up to that instead of your mama wearing mismatched sweats and screaming like a shrew to get up?

I realized I wasn't feeling stressed during the morning commute.

I was more upbeat at the office first thing.

My library card got a workout, as I took up reading a few pages of something inspirational or motivational before I left the house.

Oh, and I wrote a book.

My colleague Marshall does this, either working or working out in the wee hours. He's my hero, as his days start at 4.

I'm good with 5 or 5:30 most days. I still want to get up early on Saturdays, and I might allow myself to loll around in bed until 7 on Sundays.

So here is my secret. I start my days out right. What starts well tends to go well, and what starts badly tends to go worse, so start your day happy. Here are my tips for getting that day off to a great start:

Get a decent amount of sleep. Go to sleep in the same day you woke up in. For most people, seven to eight hours is optimum.

Set that alarm early. I know you all are about ready to toss this book at the thought of getting up at 0-dark-hundred, but give it a try. Get up at least two hours before you need to leave your house in the morning. The amount of stress you lose and good morning mood you'll gain is worth the small price of thirty minutes to an hour of sleep.

Don't get up immediately. Sounds crazy, I know, but stay with me. The day starts when you open your eyes in bed, so start your good mood there. Stretch. Think of all the blessings in your life and all the good things you will enjoy that day. Pray. Meditate. Set your intentions for the day in your mind.

Before your feet hit the floor, you will already be in a positive mindset, and because you have set that alarm early, you have the time to think, pray, count your blessings and set your day's agenda.

Think grateful thoughts. Everyone has something to be thankful for, and most of us have more than we can say grace over in the blessings department. Be thankful for your children, your spouse, your job, your car, your home, your bed, your health. If you wake up being thankful, you can't help but be happy.

Get the "Me Time" in. Mothers have an awful time getting time for themselves. For years, I really had no "Me Time" except for eating, sleeping and potty breaks, and ladies, that is no way to go through life.

Time management experts love to tell the story of filling a jar with rocks, pebbles, sand and water. The metaphor goes that if you put your big priorities, your big rocks, in the jar first, then the rest fits in.

My bad on not making my "Me Time" a big rock. I realized that if I was to survive as a single parent of four, I was going to have to make time for myself. Take care of that big rock first thing in the morning – get in your "Me Time" first thing.

Remember, you have time because you've gotten up earlier. Enjoy a cup of coffee as you watch the sun come up. (A hint on the coffee: I program my coffee maker the night before so the java is waiting on me in the a.m.!) Read. Go for a run or put on an exercise DVD. Paint your toenails. Whatever you want to do – it's your "Me Time."

Get in the bathroom first. I have a two-bathroom house and also a two-teenager house. My mornings are so much less stressful if I am up before the kids because I don't have to fight for bathroom space. I can take my time getting dressed, brushing my hair and, as my mama used to say, putting my face on. And then when everyone else is up, they see you put together. How pleasant is that?

Make breakfast. Some people hate the idea of eating breakfast. I am not one of those people. I wake up famished. If you wake up early enough, there's time to pop some muffins in the oven. Making scrambled eggs, an omelet or a soft-boiled egg is quick and easy. Or make cheese toast or a bowl of cereal. Start your day off right, and a plus is that your family will wake up to a healthy breakfast. And when someone has left a box of doughnuts on the coffee bar at work, I am not as tempted. I didn't say I wouldn't be tempted, because we know that would be a bald-faced lie.

Exercise. This is one I am working on, because I am not big on getting up to exercise. I tend to enjoy moving around in the afternoon and evening, but that's just me. The author and motivational speaker Jack Canfield advocated having a "power hour" during which 20 minutes would be spent visualizing goals, 20 minutes would be spent reading inspirational or motivational books, and 20 minutes would be spent exercising.

That's what I am going for. Just 20 minutes in the morning. There are workout tapes that are 20 minutes long or shorter. Some are even 10 minutes. You can walk a mile in 15 minutes. So you don't have to have a huge amount of time to make progress. Do your moving around first thing, and it's a big rock in the jar called "your day."

Leave with enough time to get there. This is an issue I battle, because I am one of those last-minute people. "Oh, let me start the dishwasher before I go," I think. Or fold the towels or pick up clutter.

In *The Simpsons* movie, there was a scene in which the family was fleeing their house, which was on fire. Marge is running out of the kitchen, trying to escape with her life, and she stops to wash a dish. I totally identified with that move.

Plus I like to see my children off on the bus, and our house is one of the later houses on the route, so I consciously decide to push it on time. The Boss Man at the office isn't always thrilled that I am late to meetings first thing, but I'm fortunate that he's a forgiving guy.

But here is the thing: I leave knowing I will get to the office about 10 minutes late. I don't leave late and think I will drive like Danica Patrick on the interstate to get there on time.

Fast driving, stressful driving, unsafe driving – all of that is forbidden. The drive takes the time it takes.

Use your commute. The speaker Jim Rohn talks of turning your car into a university. I don't think you can get your Ph.D. in there, but libraries have shelves and shelves of books on CDs. Listen to those, or your favorite radio station or your favorite music mix. Sing out loud – LOUD. Whatever starts your day off right, and in reverse, whatever puts you in a good mood on the way home.

I can't guarantee the rest of your day will be great. It may be lousy. Those do happen.

But I can tell you that your day has a whole lot better chance of being a good one if you start it out in a good mood. Bad moods and rushing around can turn a fantastic day bad in nothing flat.

Lolling around in bed will only get you a crazy morning with hollering, racing around and no peace.

Wake up already, but do what our mamas told us to do. Rise and shine.

Try it and you'll think lolling around is sleeping past 6:30.

Take the leaps

Bungee jumping, statistics show, is just about as dangerous as driving 100 miles in a car. We do that all the time, hopping in the car to drive 60 miles an hour down the interstate, changing lanes while talking on the phone and texting, putting on mascara and eating breakfast.

Driving in the car doesn't scare us. Bungee-jumping, though, is something terrifying. Something nobody but an adrenaline junkie wants to do.

The world went up to 1979 without anyone thinking of the idea of bungee jumping, but between 1986 and 2002, 18 people went from yelling "Oh, my God" to meeting him while taking that leap. A lot more people died driving cars. Some 30,800 in 2012 alone, according to the National Highway Traffic Safety Administration.

Sure, more people drive than bungee jump, but that's a lot of fatalities. Putting down cell phones and coffee might improve those numbers.

Then there are injuries. According to bungee jumping statistics, women can suffer uterine prolapsed while bungee jumping. Uterine prolapsed happens when pelvic floor muscles and ligaments stretch and weaken, letting gravity take over where the uterus is concerned. It's sort of like a spontaneous hysterectomy trying to happen.

If I had a hankering to go bungee jumping, which in 48 years of living I haven't, the chance of uterine prolapse would take care of that.

Just consider yourself and your uterus, if you've got one, warned.

I like my uterus right where it is, and I've also birthed four children, and none of them were less than the high end of 8 pounds. My uterus is probably barely hanging on. Like Bonjovi sang, living on a prayer.

There's also eye trauma, blindness, back injuries, bruises and rope burns, but the statistics had me at "uterine prolapse."

It's no accident that there are more lawyers trolling for car accident cases than bungee-jumping injury lawsuits. There's a whole lot more of them.

More than 2 million in 2012. The NHTSA didn't have numbers on uterine prolapsed in car accidents, but I suppose anything is possible.

The point of all this? That risks have to be taken, whether we like it or not.

We may not be bungee jumping. Lord knows I won't be.

But we drive cars, go to work, open businesses, make investments with the retirement nest egg, go on blind dates, get married, have children. These are all risky behaviors, but so is staying in bed with the covers over your head.

Life has to be lived, and the risks are outweighed by the benefits. Will you lose money, get your heart stomped on and have your children drive you crazy? Of course. But you also could strike it rich, or at least strike it middle class. You might also be loved deeply by your soulmate. Your children will also make you incredibly proud.

There are also steps you can take to make your leaps of faith a little less injury-prone. Be particular about who you give your heart to, or where you put your money. Raise your children the best you can. Always invest in yourself and your health. Good decisions usually pay off.

There's more good than bad out there waiting to happen to you.

Take the leaps. The odds are in your favor.

Parting thoughts

Life can be many things.

Terrifying can be one of them, and that is not a bad thing. If you are going to be taking some bungee jump leaps of faith, a little terror can be a good thing if you listen to it and it helps you make good decisions. Sometimes things scare the crap out of you for a reason.

But even the good decisions, the wise choices and the turning points where a moment becomes a good life, are still scary.

Living a full and rich life means being brave, and being brave means making choices and taking steps that scare you at times.

The goals might be daring or daunting or audacious enough to be terrifying, but I would make the argument that those are exactly the kind of goals that are worth having.

Why put your best efforts, getting up early, working hard and dreaming harder, into play for something small? If you are going to think small, make the small thoughts about the steps you need to take toward your gigantic goal. Whether your goal is financial or personal, about building your success or making a friendship that will turn into a long-term relationship, small steps are the best ones to take.

Remember being a young child, taking giant steps in playground games of Simon Says? Those giant steps can be hard to take. Swing your leg forward too fast in a giant step, and you'll find yourself on the ground.

Take small steps toward big goals every day.

Another key to successful bungee jumping is to have a really strong bungee cord. Something to catch you, because the law of gravity works every time.

Whether you are leaping or taking baby steps off the edges in life, there will be down times and challenges. Make sure you have something strong to pick you back up before you hit rock bottom.

Your cord should be thick and woven from friends, family, spiritual care, keeping your body healthy and your mind sharp, learning, reading, prayer, meditation and thought. Make sure you have support from yourself and others that will save you when you need saving.

Love and money and taking risks in life can be how success is defined.

Back in the day, I was voted Most Likely to Succeed my senior year of high school. There have been plenty of times in my life when I thought that was a joke. I was working hard and going somewhere, but that somewhere was deeper in debt. I had a marriage that had more than its share of troubles during those times, and I wanted to spend more time with my children. I also wanted to get a little Annie time, because I had been using my personal time for eating and sleeping.

I was out of balance, stressed, unhealthy and had a large lack of self doubt. I didn't feel very successful. Likely or not, success did not describe where I was or what I was doing.

Am I a success now? Yes. No likely to it. I am.

Why is that? Is it because I have made better choices financially? Is it because most of the time, I am at peace with where I am in my personal life?

Love and money are part of it, but they don't define success for me.

Success is about loving what you have in life, yet reaching for more.

It's about the right now and the future, and it's about making peace with the past.

Success is about loving your family and friends not only in words but in deeds. It is about making time for the people who you hold in your heart.

Success is about balance. Too much work, and your bank balance might be higher, but the price could be your health or your relationships. Who wants to have wealth when you are too sick to enjoy it and have no one to enjoy it with?

The key to being in balance—love, money, relationships, children, health, mind and spirit--is in love and respect for yourself. When you are healthy emotionally, physically and spiritually, you bless all those you love, all you touch and everything you do with a complete and in-balance self.

I've heard this quote in North Mississippi, but turns out it was penned by Voltaire. "God gave us the gift of life; it is up to us to give ourselves the gift of living well."

Living well is also the gift we give back to God and to all who are a part of our lives.

Living a good and balanced happy life is what I call success.

Live well, and be blessed.

Acknowledgements

I would like to thank the friends, male and female, who have shown me their love by listening and by sharing their experiences and thoughts about this adventure we call life, and my children, who are and have always been my heart. Thanks also go to my colleagues and to Brian Tolley, former executive editor of *The Clarion-Ledger*, and former *Clarion-Ledger* publisher Leslie Hurst, both of whom have been mentors professionally. Gratitude also goes to Sartoris Literary Group President James L. Dickerson, who is the kind of publisher and editor every writer should have, and to Grant Phillips, who encourages me to dream the dreams and take the leaps I should.

www.ingramcontent.com/pod-product-compliance
Lightning Source LLC
LaVergne TN
LVHW041332080426
835512LV00006B/408